The Little Singapore Cookbook

WENDY HUTTON

Marshall Cavendish
Cuisine

The Little Singapore Cookbook

Copyright © 2013 Marshall Cavendish International (Asia) Private Limited
This edition with new cover © 2021

Published by Marshall Cavendish Cuisine
An imprint of Marshall Cavendish International

A member of the
Times Publishing Group

Other Marshall Cavendish Offices:
Marshall Cavendish Corporation, 800 Westchester Ave, Suite N-641, Rye Brook, NY 10573, USA •
Marshall Cavendish International (Thailand) Co Ltd, 253 Asoke, 16th Floor, Sukhumvit 21 Road,
Klongtoey Nua, Wattana, Bangkok 10110, Thailand • Marshall Cavendish (Malaysia) Sdn Bhd,
Times Subang, Lot 46, Subang Hi-Tech Industrial Park, Batu Tiga, 40000 Shah Alam,
Selangor Darul Ehsan, Malaysia

Marshall Cavendish is a registered trademark of Times Publishing Limited

National Library Board, Singapore Cataloguing-in-Publication Data

Name(s): Hutton, Wendy.
Title: The little Singapore cookbook / Wendy Hutton.
Description: Singapore : Marshall Cavendish Cuisine, [2021]
Identifier(s): OCN 1251466425 | ISBN 978-981-4974-88-2 (paperback)
Subject(s): LCSH: Cooking, Singaporean. | LCGFT: Cookbooks.
Classification: DDC 641.595957--dc23

Printed in Singapore

Contents

Introduction

In just under two centuries, Singapore has grown from a tiny backwater inhabited by a few fishermen to an international phenomenon: a dynamic, ultra-modern city state where some of the world's most striking architecture co-exists with colonial-era shophouses.

The contrast of old and new is just as evident in the food which is enjoyed in Singapore, with sophisticated and innovative cuisines from around the world joining —but never replacing in local hearts—the distinctive Singaporean cuisine.

What is it that makes Singapore's traditional food so special? Perhaps it is the result of the energy, the adaptability and the ingenuity of the immigrants who came to this Southeast Asian outpost in search of a better life. Coolies arrived in their thousands from the provinces of southern China; manual workers and traders made the long journey from India; Malays came from nearby Johore and Sumatra, joined by Bugis, Javanese, Armenians and Arabs, all bringing their traditional cuisines to the island founded as a British colony in 1819.

Over decades of culinary cohabitation, many of the dishes which originated in, say, China's Fujian province or the Indian state of Kerala, in Java or in the Arab world, gradually took on a local accent. Cooks borrowed ingredients and techniques from each other, modifying (and, many would say, improving) the original dishes of their homeland. Chillies became an essential accompaniment to many Chinese dishes; the Malays and Indians adopted Chinese soy sauce, noodles, bean curd and bean sprouts; English seasoning sauces were enthusiastically used as marinades or in dips by everyone and Middle Eastern flavourings such as rosewater crept into desserts or savoury rice dishes.

Intermarriage, too, helped change what was coming out of the woks and clay cooking pots of Singapore. The overwhelming majority of the early migrants were Chinese men, and a number of them, including Chinese traders who moved to Singapore from other British settlements in nearby Malacca and Penang, married Malay or Javanese women. Over the years, this produced a distinctive blending of Chinese and Malay customs, language and cuisine known as Peranakan culture.

The cuisine of the Peranakan women, known as Nyonya, is a distinctively Singapore cuisine, as is the food of the Eurasians, the descendants of intermarriage between Europeans and Asians.

The favourite foods of Singapore are prepared by cooks rather than chefs, honest dishes which have stood the test of time and are still enjoyed in Singaporean homes, in simple restaurants or coffee shops, and at stalls in food or hawker centres.

This book brings together some of the best-loved dishes of Singapore. Noodles are perhaps the all-time favourite, whether they're the iconic southern Chinese fried Hokkien noodles or Thai-inspired *mee siam*, Singapore's unique spicy noodle soup, *laksa lemak*, or a dish you'll never find in India, Indian *mee goreng*. And when it comes to breads, you'll find recipes for meat-filled *murtabak*, an Indian Muslim dish, as well as *roti* John, spicy meat sandwiched in a French loaf and doused with tomato sauce. And who could overlook the favourite *roti prata*, a Singaporean take on Indian griddle-cooked bread, light, flaky and utterly satisfying when dipped into curry gravy or simmered lentils. No Asian cuisine is without its rice dishes, and Singapore's favourites include coconut-rich *nasi lemak* and the ever-versatile *nasi goreng*.

Local seafood dishes include fish head curry, created in Singapore by a cook from southern India, and spicy, well-loved chilli crab and black pepper crab. Regardless of their ethnic original, all Singaporeans love to eat traditional Malay chicken curry and coconut-rich beef *rendang*, as well as the famous barbecued meat skewers, satay.

Singaporeans cannot resist snack foods, and regardless of their ethnic origin, enthuse over curry puffs and the wonderful Hokkien roll known as *popiah*. And who could resist the naughty but oh-so-nice batter-coated deep-fried bananas or *goreng pisang*? Or the inviting green-coloured Malay pancake rolls, *kuih dadar*, filled with grated coconut sweetened with palm sugar?

This book contains some of my favourite Singapore foods, dishes which I have been preparing and enjoying for the past 45 years, and ones which I feel will delight anyone with a love of really good food.

Wendy Hutton

Noodles, Rice & Breads

Kon Loh Mee *8*

Fried Hokkien Noodles *11*

Char Kway Teow *12*

Beehoon Soup *15*

Indian Mee Goreng *16*

Laksa Lemak *18*

Mee Rebus *21*

Mee Siam *22*

Soto Ayam *24*

Nasi Lemak *27*

Nasi Goreng *28*

Hainanese Chicken Rice *30*

Clay Pot Chicken and Rice *33*

Chicken Biryani *34*

Gado Gado *37*

Roti John *38*

Roti Prata *41*

Murtabak *42*

Kon Loh Mee Serves 4

A simple version of these noodles prepared with just the seasoning sauces, is popular for breakfast in the coffee shops. For a more substantial meal, however, this recipe includes some green vegetables, black mushrooms and Chinese red roasted pork.

2 teaspoons peanut or vegetable oil

4 teaspoons sesame oil

4 teaspoons dark soy sauce

4 teaspoons chilli sauce

400 g fresh wheat flour noodles or dried egg noodles

6–8 stalks Chinese flowering cabbage (*choy sum* or *chye sim*), cut into 5-cm lengths and blanched in boiling water

2–3 dried black mushrooms, soaked in hot water to soften, simmered until soft and caps sliced

150–200 g Chinese red roasted pork (*char siew*), sliced

pickled green chillies, to taste

1. Combine both lots of oil, soy sauce and chilli sauce in a large bowl and set aside.

2. If using fresh noodles, shake the noodles in a colander to dislodge any starch. Heat a large pan of water and when it is boiling vigorously, add the fresh or dried noodles and cook until done; fresh noodles need less than 1 minute. Transfer the noodles to a colander, drain and rinse briefly with fresh water. Plunge back into the boiling water for a few seconds, drain again, then add to the bowl of sauces.

3. Add the cabbage, mushrooms and pork and toss to mix well.

4. Divide among 4 plates and serve with a condiment of pickled green chillies, if desired.

You'll find a jar of pickled green chillies on almost every coffee shop table in Singapore. Tangy yet not fiery hot, they are put into a small bowl with soy sauce and eaten as an accompaniment to noodles and rice dishes. To make your own, slice 10 large green chillies and place in a heatproof screw-top jar. Add $1/2$ cup (125 ml) boiling water and $1/2$ cup (125 ml) vinegar. Leave to cool to room temperature before closing the jar. Let stand at room temperature for about 3 days before using. The chillies can be kept for several months if refrigerated.

Fried Hokkien Noodles Serves 6–8

Probably Singapore's best-loved noodle dish, this consists of thick fresh yellow noodles and rice vermicelli, combined with boiled pork, prawns and bean sprouts. You can also add some squid for an even richer flavour.

500 g fresh thick yellow (Hokkien) noodles

150 g dried rice vermicelli, soaked in hot water to soften, cut into 8-cm lengths

250 g belly pork, simmered until cooked, stock reserved, meat thinly sliced

3 tablespoons vegetable oil

300 g small prawns, peeled and deveined, heads and shells reserved, or 150 g prawns and 150 g cleaned, sliced squid

8–10 cloves garlic, smashed and finely chopped

2 eggs, lightly beaten

250 g bean sprouts, washed and drained, tails removed

1 teaspoon salt

$1/4$ teaspoon white pepper

25 g Chinese chives or spring onions, cut into 2-cm lengths

sambal belacan (page 27)

4 small round green limes (limau kasturi), stalk ends sliced off, or 1 lime, quartered

1. Put the fresh thick yellow noodles in a bowl and pour boiling water over. Stand 1 minute, then drain in a colander and combine with the soaked and drained rice vermicelli.

2. Measure the reserved pork stock and add water if required to make 1 cup (250 ml) liquid. Set aside.

3. Heat 1 tablespoon oil in a saucepan and stir-fry the prawn heads and shells until they turn pink. Add the reserved pork stock to the prawn shells, bring to the boil, cover and simmer for 5 minutes. Strain, pressing down on the prawn shells with the back of a spoon to extract as much liquid as possible. Return the stock to the pan, add the prawns and squid, if using, and simmer for 2–3 minutes until just cooked. Strain and reserve the stock, prawns and squid separately. (The recipe can be prepared in advance up to this stage, and all ingredients refrigerated for several hours.)

4. Heat the remaining 2 tablespoons oil in a wok and stir-fry the garlic until it turns golden brown and flavours the oil. Discard the garlic and increase the heat. When the oil is very hot, pour in the beaten eggs and stir for 1 minute.

5. Add the noodles, bean sprouts and $1/2$ cup (125 ml) reserved stock. Stir-fry over high heat for 1 minute, then add the pork, prawns, salt and pepper. Stir-fry for 2–3 minutes until everything is heated through and well mixed, adding a little more stock if the noodles threaten to stick.

6. Add the Chinese chives, stir for a few seconds, then transfer to a large serving dish. Serve with sambal belacan and limes, or, if desired, small bowls of dark soy sauce with sliced red chillies.

Char Kway Teow Serves 6–8

Another classic Singapore noodle dish, this Teochew creation includes tiny fried dice of pork fat—naughty in these health-conscious days, but oh so nice! You can omit these if you like, but the dish won't taste the same.

100 g hard pork fat (cut from the back), cut into 1-cm cubes

2 tablespoons water

4 cloves garlic, smashed and chopped

2 large red chillies, crushed to a paste

200 g lean pork, shredded

400 g raw prawns, peeled and deveined

200 g squid, cleaned and sliced

1 tablespoon light soy sauce

1 tablespoon dark soy sauce

2 teaspoons oyster sauce

$1/2$ teaspoon salt

a liberal sprinkling of white pepper

250 g bean sprouts, washed and drained, tails removed

1 kg fresh flat rice flour noodles (*kway teow*), scalded in boiling water, rinsed and drained

1 large red chilli, sliced

sprigs of coriander leaves to garnish

1. Put the pork fat and water in a wok and cook over medium heat, stirring from time to time, until the water has evaporated and oil runs out, turning the pieces of fat golden and crisp. Remove and drain on paper towels. Leave 3 tablespoons pork oil in the wok and discard the remainder.

2. Heat the pork oil and stir-fry the garlic and chilli over low–medium heat for about 30 seconds. Increase the heat, add the pork and stir-fry for 2 minutes. Add the prawns and squid, then stir-fry for 2 minutes. Season with both lots of soy sauce, oyster sauce, salt and pepper.

3. Add the bean sprouts and stir-fry for 1 minute, then put in the rice flour noodles and stir-fry until well mixed and heated through. Stir in the crisp pork fat and transfer to a serving dish. Garnish with chilli and coriander leaves.

If you prefer to omit the pork oil, use 3 tablespoons vegetable oil for frying.

Beehoon Soup Serves 6

There are countless versions of soup containing rice vermicelli or *beehoon* in Singapore. Some of the more popular versions add fish balls or, in the case of a Hakka favourite, *yong tau foo*, a variety of vegetables and various types of bean curd stuffed with fish paste. This recipe includes pork, prawns, fish balls and fish cakes, although you could easily omit one or two of these ingredients and increase the portion of those you've selected.

250 g lean pork, in one piece

7 cups (1.75 litres) pork or chicken stock

400 g dried rice vermicelli (*beehoon*), soaked to soften

200 g bean sprouts washed and drained, tails removed

1 small bunch of Chinese flowering cabbage (*chye sim* or *choy sum*) or spinach, cut into 5-cm lengths, blanched

1 tablespoon vegetable oil

250 g prawns, peeled, heads and shells reserved

24 small fish balls

1–2 fried fish cakes, sliced

salt to taste

1–2 spring onions, finely chopped

crisp-fried shallots to garnish

white pepper to taste

1. Put the pork into a saucepan with the stock. Bring to the boil, lower the heat and simmer with the pan covered until the meat is tender. Remove the meat, slice thinly and set aside.

2. Put the rice vermicelli into a saucepan of boiling water and simmer until just cooked but still firm, separating the noodles as they start to soften. Drain and divide the cooked vermicelli among 6 large bowls. Add the bean sprouts and cooked vegetables to each portion. Set aside.

3. Heat the oil in a saucepan and add the prawn heads and shells. Stir-fry until they turn pink, then add the pork stock. Bring to the boil, cover and simmer for 30 minutes. Strain, pressing down on the prawn shells with the back of a spoon to extract the liquid. Return the strained stock to the pan, bring to the boil and add the peeled prawns. Simmer for 2–3 minutes until just cooked, then divide the prawns among the soup bowls.

4. Add the fish balls to the pan and simmer for 10 minutes, then add the fish cake and simmer for 1–2 minutes until heated through, then add salt to taste. Put some of the soup, fish balls and fish cakes in each bowl, then sprinkle with spring onions, crisp-fried shallots and white pepper. Serve hot with sauce bowls of sliced red chilli in light soy sauce, if desired.

Should you not be able to find fish balls in your market or supermarket, here's a recipe for making them at home—really easy with a food processor. Skin and debone 500 g fine white-fleshed fish such as wolf herring (*ikan parang*), Spanish mackerel (*ikan tenggiri*), sea bass or snapper. Cut the fish into cubes, making certain all bones and skin have been discarded. Put in a food processor and pulse until the fish is coarsely minced. Add 1/2 teaspoon salt, a liberal sprinkling of white pepper and 1 teaspoon cornflour and pulse a few more times. With the processor on high speed, add 4 tablespoons iced water slowly and process until you achieve a smooth paste. To shape into balls, put the mixture in a bowl and wet your hands. Take a handful of the mixture and squeeze through your thumb and forefinger, using a spoon to scrape off a sizeable lump. The resulting fish balls should be about 2 cm in diameter. Soak the fish balls in salted water (1 teaspoon salt per 2 cups / 500 ml water) and refrigerate until required.

Indian Mee Goreng Serves 4–5

You won't find this dish in India, as it is a Singaporean creation using Chinese ingredients such as noodles and bean curd with Indian curry leaves and Western tomato sauce. It sounds like a hodge-podge, but it works brilliantly. And it's ideal for vegetarians too.

500 g fresh thick yellow (Hokkien) noodles

4 tablespoons vegetable oil

1 medium red or brown-skinned onion, chopped

12–16 curry leaves, finely chopped

1 ripe tomato, finely chopped

2 tablespoons chopped garlic chives or spring onions

2–3 tablespoons tomato sauce

1 tablespoon chilli sauce

1 tablespoon light soy sauce

2 eggs, lightly beaten

1 medium potato, boiled, peeled and cut into 1-cm cubes

1 piece (about 100 g) firm bean curd, dried with paper towels, cut into 1-cm cubes and deep-fried until golden brown

1 large green chilli, thinly sliced

1. Put the noodles into a colander and rinse under warm running water. Drain thoroughly and set aside.

2. Heat the oil in a wok, then add the onion and curry leaves and stir-fry over medium heat for about 4 minutes until soft. Add the drained noodles, tomato, chives or spring onions, tomato sauce, chilli sauce and soy sauce and stir-fry over medium heat for 3 minutes, mixing well.

3. Pour the beaten egg over the noodles and leave to set, then mix in with the noodles. Add the potato and bean curd and stir-fry for about 1 minute to heat through.

4. Transfer the noodles to a large serving dish and scatter the sliced green chilli on top. Serve hot with additional tomato and chilli sauce, for adding to taste, if desired.

Laksa Lemak Serves 6

Unlike the sour, fishy *laksa* of Penang, Singapore's version of this noodle dish is coconut milk-rich and has all kinds of fragrant seasonings. The name *laksa* comes from the Hokkien term, *luak sua*, meaning spicy sand, with the abundant ground dried prawns giving the gravy its almost sandy texture. This recipe is time-consuming so it's a good idea to make it the central dish at a *laksa* party. The amounts given serve six, but can easily be doubled.

2 large fried fish cakes, blanched in boiling water, thinly sliced

6 deep-fried brown bean curd (*tau pok*), blanched in boiling water for 1 minute, sliced

1.25 kg fresh round rice flour (*laska*) noodles, blanched in boiling water for 30 seconds and drained, or 500 g dried rice-flour (*laksa*) noodles or dried rice vermicelli (*beehoon*), prepared according to package instructions

250 g bean sprouts, washed and drained, tails removed

600 g prawns, simmered in water to cover, peeled and deveined (stock reserved)

18 hard-boiled quail eggs, peeled and halved, or 3 hard-boiled hen eggs, peeled and quartered

6 tablespoons finely chopped polygonum leaves (*daun kesom*) to garnish

6 small green limes (*limau kasturi*), stalk ends sliced off, or 1 lime, quartered

LAKSA GRAVY

15–20 dried chillies, cut into 2-cm lengths, soaked in hot water to soften, some seeds discarded if preferred

3–4 large red chillies, sliced

25 (about 250 g) shallots, chopped

8-cm knob galangal, chopped

8 cloves garlic, chopped

4-cm knob ginger, chopped

4 stems lemon grass, tender inner part of bottom 10 cm only, sliced

4-cm knob fresh turmeric, chopped or 1 teaspoon turmeric powder

4 candlenuts, crushed

2 1/4 teaspoons dried shrimp paste

1/4 cup (125 ml) vegetable oil

1 1/4 tablespoons coriander powder

50 g dried prawns, lightly toasted in a dry wok, ground to a powder

water, as needed

6 large sprigs polygonum leaves (*daun kesom*)

2 teaspoons salt, or more to taste

2 teaspoon sugar, or more to taste

6 cups (1.5 litres) coconut milk

CHILLI SAMBAL

6 dried chillies, cut into 2-cm lengths, soaked to soften

6 large red chillies, sliced

1 1/4 teaspoons dried shrimp paste

1/4 teaspoon salt

1/4 teaspoon sugar

3 tablespoons water

1/4 cup (65 ml) vegetable oil

1. Prepare the *laksa* gravy in advance. Process both lots of chillies, shallots, galangal, garlic, ginger, lemon grass, turmeric, candlenuts and shrimp paste to a smooth paste, adding a little oil if required to keep the mixture turning.

2. Heat the oil in a very large saucepan or terracotta pot (*chatty*), add the chilli paste and stir-fry over low-moderate heat until fragrant and the oil starts to separate, 10–15 minutes. Add the coriander powder and stir-fry for 1 minute. Add the dried prawns and stir-fry for 1 minute. Measure the reserved prawn stock

and add water to make 6 cups (1.5 litres) liquid. Add liquid to the pan with the polygonum leaves, salt and sugar. Bring to the boil, lower heat and simmer uncovered for 10 minutes. Add the coconut milk, bring gently to the boil, stirring, then simmer for 5 minutes. Add the blanched fish cake and bean curd and simmer for about 1 minute to heat through. Turn off the heat, taste and adjust salt and sugar if required. Discard the polygonum leaves.

3. While the *laksa* gravy is simmering, prepare the chilli sambal. Process both lots of chillies, shrimp paste, salt and sugar to make a smooth paste, adding the water gradually. Heat the oil in a small pan and add the paste. Stir-fry over low heat until cooked and the oil separates from the mixture, 6–8 minutes. Cool and serve in small sauce bowls, with a cut lime or lime wedges on each.

4. To complete the *laksa*, divide the noodles, rice vermicelli and bean sprouts among 6 large bowls. Fill each bowl with hot gravy, dividing the fish cakes and deep-fried bean curd evenly. Top with prawns and eggs. Garnish with chopped polygonum leaves and serve immediately with chilli sambal and limes.

Mee Rebus Serves 4

One of the secrets to the excellent flavour of this Malay noodle dish is the rich meaty gravy thickened with sweet potato.

250 g beef topside, in one piece

2 cups (500 ml) water

1/2 teaspoon salt

1/2 teaspoon freshly ground black pepper

1 stalk Chinese celery with leaves

400 g fresh thick yellow (Hokkien) noodles

160 g bean sprouts, washed and drained, tails removed

2–3 hard-boiled eggs, peeled and quartered

4 tablespoons deep-fried shallots

4 tablespoons chopped Chinese celery leaves

1 lime, quartered

GRAVY

3 candlenuts, crushed

6 shallots, chopped

2 thin slices galangal, chopped

2–3 large red chillies, sliced

2–4 teaspoons chilli paste (sambal olek)

2 tablespoons vegetable oil

1 1/2 teaspoons coriander powder

1 1/2 teaspoons salted soy beans (tau cheo), mashed

1/2 cup mashed boiled sweet potato

1. Put the beef in a saucepan with water, salt, pepper and Chinese celery. Bring to the boil, cover and simmer until the beef is tender, about 1 1/4 hours. Drain, reserving the stock, and cut the beef into 1-cm cubes.

2. To make the gravy, process the candlenuts, shallots, galangal and both lots of chillies in a spice grinder until fine. Heat oil in a saucepan and gently stir-fry the processed mixture for 3 minutes. Add the coriander powder and salted soy beans and stir-fry for 2 minutes. Add the sweet potato, then gradually stir in the reserved stock to make a thick gravy. Add the meat cubes and heat through.

3. Blanch the noodles in a large saucepan of boiling water for just 1 minute. Drain and divide among 4 large bowls. Divide the bean sprouts among the bowls, then ladle the meat with gravy over each portion.

4. Garnish with eggs, deep-fried shallots, chopped celery leaves and a piece of lime. Serve hot.

Mee Siam Serves 4

A Nyonya classic, *mee siam* or Siamese noodles has the distinctive hot, sweet and sour flavours of Thai cuisine. This more elaborate version of a hawker favourite takes some time to prepare, so it is a dish for special occasions.

160 g bean sprouts, washed and drained, tails removed

25 g Chinese chives, cut into 2-cm lengths

300 g cooked prawns, peeled, heads removed, halved lengthways if large

300 g dried rice vermicelli (*beehoon*), soaked in hot water to soften, drained and cut into 6-cm lengths

1 piece (100–125 g) hard bean curd, deep-fried until golden, halved crossways and thinly sliced

2 hard-boiled eggs, peeled and quartered

2 limes, quartered, or 8 small round green limes (*limau kasturi*), halved

SPICE PASTE

8–10 dried chillies, soaked to soften, some seeds discarded if less spicy taste preferred

8 shallots, chopped

6 candlenuts, crushed

$1/4$ cup (60 ml) vegetable oil

$1/4$ cup salted soy beans (*tau cheo*), lightly crushed with the back of a spoon

3–4 teaspoons sugar

GRAVY

4 cups (1 litre) water

3 tablespoons dried prawns, soaked to soften, blended to a powder

2 heaped tablespoons tamarind pulp, soaked in $1/2$ cup (125 ml) warm water, squeezed and strained for juice

CHILLI SAMBAL

6 dried chillies, cut into 2-cm lengths, soaked to soften

6 large red chillies, sliced

$1^1/4$ teaspoons dried shrimp paste

$1/4$ teaspoon salt

$1/4$ teaspoon sugar

3 tablespoons water

$1/4$ cup (65 ml) vegetable oil

1. Prepare the spice paste by grinding the chillies, shallots and candlenuts in a spice grinder, adding a little oil if required to keep the blades turning. Heat the oil in a wok then add the spice paste and stir-fry over low–medium heat for 3–4 minutes, stirring frequently, until fragrant. Add the salted soy beans and stir-fry for 30 seconds, then sprinkle in sugar and cook another 30 seconds. Remove half the spice paste from the wok.

2. To prepare the gravy, put the spice paste you have removed from the wok into a large saucepan, leaving the remainder in the wok for frying the rice vermicelli. Add the water and dried prawn powder to the saucepan, bring to the boil, then add the tamarind juice. Simmer for 3 minutes, remove from the heat but keep the gravy in the saucepan.

3. Heat the remaining spice paste in the wok, then add the bean sprouts and stir-fry over high heat for 30 seconds. Add half the Chinese chives and half the prawns and stir-fry for 30 seconds. Add the rice vermicelli, a little at a time, stirring vigorously to mix it thoroughly with the other ingredients. Stir-fry for 2 minutes, then transfer to a large serving dish.

4. Arrange the remaining Chinese chives and prawns on top of the rice vermicelli and garnish with the bean curd, eggs and limes. Re-heat the gravy, transfer to a deep bowl or jug and serve hot. Alternatively, divide the vermicelli, Chinese chives, prawns, bean curd and eggs among 4 large bowls, topping each up with gravy, accompanied with limes and chilli sambal.

Soto Ayam Serves 4

This is Indonesian in origin and a favourite lunch dish or snack. If you have time, you can add potato cakes (*pergedel*) or simply use sliced boiled potatoes. *Pergedel* (from the Dutch *frikkadel*) are savoury fritters commonly made with potatoes or corn in Indonesia.

500 g chicken pieces, bone left in

5 cups (1.25 litres) water

1 teaspoon salt

1 stem lemon grass, bruised and cut into 3–4 pieces

1 cup (250 ml) coconut milk

1 kaffir lime leaf (*daun limau purut*)

100 g dried rice vermicelli (*beehoon*) or transparent mung bean noodles, soaked to soften, drained and cut into 8-cm lengths

4 *pergedel* or 1–2 waxy potatoes, peeled, boiled and sliced

1 heaped cup (100 g) bean sprouts, washed and drained, tails removed

a few spinach leaves, blanched and coarsely chopped

1–2 hard-boiled eggs, peeled and sliced

1–2 tablespoons crisp-fried shallots

coriander leaves

SEASONING

1 teaspoon black peppercorns

1 teaspoon coriander seeds

4 candlenuts, crushed

2 cloves garlic, chopped

6 shallots, chopped

1 slice ginger, chopped

$1/4$ teaspoon turmeric powder

2 tablespoons vegetable oil

PERGEDEL (OPTIONAL)

500 g unpeeled floury potatoes

$1/2$ teaspoon salt

$1/4$ teaspoon freshly ground black pepper

2 spring onions, finely chopped

1 large green chilli, finely chopped

$1/3$ cup crisp-fried shallots

vegetable oil for deep-frying

1 egg, lightly beaten

1. Put the chicken, water, salt and lemon grass in a pan. Bring to the boil, cover, lower heat and simmer until the chicken is tender. Remove the chicken, cool slightly, then shred the meat. Discard the lemon grass but save the cooking liquid.

2. Prepare the seasoning. Process the peppercorns and coriander seeds to a powder in a spice grinder, then add all the other ingredients except the oil and process to a smooth paste, adding a little oil, if required, to keep the blades turning. Heat the oil in a heavy pan and add the ground ingredients. Stir-fry over low–medium heat for about 4 minutes until fragrant, then add the reserved chicken stock. Bring to the boil, cover, lower the heat and simmer for 5 minutes. Add the coconut milk and lime leaf and simmer with the pan uncovered for 5 minutes. Add noodles and simmer for 30 seconds.

3. To serve, divide the noodles, chicken, *pergedel* or potato slices, bean sprouts, spinach and eggs among 4 large bowls, topping each up with chicken stock. Garnish with shallots and coriander leaves.

4. To make *pergedel*, bring a large saucepan of water to the boil. Add the whole potatoes, cover the saucepan and boil for 15–20 minutes, until the potatoes are tender when pierced with a skewer. Drain, cool and peel the potatoes, then mash coarsely.

5. Add salt, pepper, spring onion, chilli and crisp-fried shallots and stir to mix well. Take about one-third cup of the mixture and roll it into a ball between your wet palms, pressing

firmly so that the mixture will hold its shape during frying. Flatten each ball to form a circle about 2 cm thick. Put the potato cakes on a plate and cover with plastic wrap. Refrigerate for at least 30 minutes.

6. Heat oil for deep-frying. When the oil is very hot, dip a potato cake into the beaten egg, letting the excess egg drain off, then use a slotted spatula to slide the potato cake into the hot oil. Fry up to 4 potato cakes at the same time. Cook for about $1^1/_2$ minutes, turning over when they are golden brown underneath and cook the other side until golden brown. Remove the potato cakes and drain on paper towels. Serve hot.

Nasi Lemak Serves 4

Nasi lemak or rich rice is cooked in coconut milk. The same name is given to the popular combination—generally served at breakfast—of coconut rice, cucumber, egg, crunchy deep-fried fish or peanuts and a chilli sambal. You could either serve the coconut rice as an accompaniment to almost any Malay meal, or try it with some of the traditional accompaniments below.

2¹/₂ cups (625 ml) coconut milk

1 teaspoon salt

2 fresh or dried pandan leaves, tied into a knot (optional)

400 g long-grain rice, washed and drained

ACCOMPANIMENTS

2 eggs, lightly beaten, cooked to make a thin omelette, shredded

100 g salted roasted peanuts

¹/₃ small cucumber, skin raked with a fork, sliced

SAMBAL BELACAN

1¹/₂ teaspoons dried shrimp paste

5–6 large red chillies, sliced

¹/₄ teaspoon salt, or more to taste

1. Put the coconut milk, salt and pandan leaves, if using, in a heavy saucepan. Bring to the boil over low–medium heat, stirring constantly. Pour in the rice, stir, then partially cover with the lid. Cook over low heat for about 5 minutes, until coconut milk is completely absorbed. Wipe the inside of the lid, then cover the pan firmly, remove from heat and leave to stand for 5 minutes.

2. Wipe the saucepan lid again, cover the pan and put back over very low heat to cook for 15 minutes. Remove the pan from the heat, fluff up the rice with a fork, cover and let stand until required, for at least 10 minutes. Remove pandan leaves before serving.

3. If serving with accompaniments, divide the rice among 4 plates and add some of the omelette, peanuts, cucumber and *sambal belacan* to each portion. Serve hot. To prepare the *sambal belacan*, toast the dried shrimp paste and while it is still hot, grind it with the chillies and salt until the chillies are finely ground but not turned into a smooth paste.

Nasi Goreng Serves 6–8

Not surprisingly, Malay-style fried rice tends to be spicier than Chinese versions, and meat or chicken is often replaced with dried anchovies, salted fish or fresh prawns; some cooks even add a spoonful of raisins for a touch of sweetness.

8 shallots, chopped

4 cloves garlic, chopped

2–3 large red chillies, chopped

$1/4$ cup (60 ml) vegetable oil

250 g small prawns, peeled and deveined

6 cups cold cooked rice, stirred with a fork
    to separate grains

1 teaspoon salt

2 eggs, cooked to make a thin omelette, shredded

2–3 tablespoons deep-fried shallots to garnish

1 sprig Chinese celery leaves, chopped,
    or 1 spring onion, thinly sliced

1. Process or pound the shallots, garlic and chillies to a paste, adding a little oil if required to keep the blades turning.

2. Heat a wok for 30 seconds, then add the oil. When moderately hot, add the ground mixture and stir-fry for 30 seconds. Add the prawns and stir-fry until they change colour.

3. Increase the heat to maximum, then add the rice and salt. Stir-fry for about 2 minutes until well mixed and the rice is heated through.

4. Transfer to a serving dish and garnish with omelette, deep-fried shallots and celery leaves or spring onion. Serve hot.

Hainanese Chicken Rice Serves 4–6

This simple but satisfying chicken dish is so strongly associated with Singapore that in neighbouring countries, it is referred to as Singapore chicken rice. The chicken is always served with special rice, light chicken soup, sliced cucumber and a chilli-ginger dip. The chicken, which must be fresh, not frozen, is cooked by steeping rather than simmering. Although more time-consuming, the steeping method produces a much better textured chicken.

1 fresh chicken (1.25–1.5 kg), excess fat removed

1 teaspoon Chinese rice wine, preferably Shao Hsing

1 1/2 tablespoons light soy sauce

2 slices ginger

1 clove garlic, bruised but left whole

1 spring onion, chopped

1 teaspoon sesame oil

1/4 teaspoon salt

shredded lettuce, sliced cucumber to garnish

coriander leaves to garnish (optional)

dark soy sauce to taste

RICE

400 g long-grain rice

sufficient chicken stock to cover rice by a height of 2 cm

a small piece of chicken fat (1–2 teaspoons)

CHILLI-GINGER SAUCE

8–10 large red chillies, chopped

1 large clove garlic, chopped

2-cm knob ginger, chopped

2 teaspoons chicken stock (from simmering chicken)

1/4 teaspoon salt

GINGER DIPPING SAUCE

2-cm knob ginger, chopped

3 teaspoons water

1 teaspoon white vinegar

1. Remove the fat from the top of the cavity of the chicken and reserve for cooking the rice. Rub the cavity with rice wine and 1/2 tablespoon light soy sauce. Tuck in the ginger, garlic and spring onion, reserving enough to make 1 tablespoon of finely chopped spring onion for the soup.

2. Choose a pan just large enough to hold the chicken and sufficient water to cover the chicken. Add water and when boiling rapidly, turn off the heat and add the chicken, ensuring that it is immersed in the water. Cover the pan and let the chicken steep for 5 minutes. Lift the chicken and drain the water from the stomach cavity back into the pan, then return the chicken to the water, cover the pan and stand for 15 minutes. Repeat the draining process and steep for another 10 minutes.

3. Turn on the heat and bring the water almost to the boil. Turn off the heat and let the chicken steep for 15 minutes. Lift the chicken, drain out the water, then steep for another 15 minutes. The chicken is now cooked.

4. While the chicken is cooking, prepare the rice by putting it in a pan with the stock and chicken fat. Bring quickly to the boil, lower the heat and simmer with the pan half covered until the water is entirely absorbed. Lower the heat to the minimum, cover the pan and cook for 10 minutes. Fluff up the rice with a fork and remove from heat.

5. Prepare the chilli-ginger sauce and ginger dipping sauce separately by processing all the ingredients in a spice grinder or blender until finely ground. Transfer to individual sauce bowls.

6. To prepare the soup, heat the liquid in which the chicken was cooked, adding a little chicken stock powder or a stock cube to intensify the flavour. Serve in small bowls garnished with some of the reserved spring onion.

7. To serve the chicken, cut into bite-size pieces; it is normally served at room temperature but can be served hot or warm. Combine the remaining 1 tablespoon light soy sauce with sesame oil and salt, and drizzle over the chicken pieces. Divide the chicken pieces into individual portions and arrange on small plates lined with beds of lettuce.

8. Garnish with sliced cucumber. Scoop the rice into individual bowls and serve with each portion of meat together with small dishes of dark soy sauce, chilli-ginger sauce and ginger dipping sauce.

9. Alternatively, serve the rice together with the meat on the same plate as follows: lightly grease the inside of a rice bowl and fill with the cooked rice, pressing down slightly. Turn upside down over a serving plate and ease out to make a mound. Repeat to make 4 mounds of rice on separate plates. Add chicken pieces and some cucumber to each serving and garnish with sprigs of coriander leaves, if using. Serve with soup, sauce bowls of dark soy sauce, chilli-ginger sauce and ginger dipping sauce.

Clay Pot Chicken and Rice Serves 4–6

Coarse clay pots (also known as sandy pots, because of their colour and texture) with a brown glaze inside are favoured for cooking a range of home-style Southern Chinese dishes. This combination of chicken, mushrooms, Chinese sausages and rice is real comfort food. If you can't get a proper clay pot (they're widely available in Chinese stores internationally), use any other heatproof ceramic or cast iron casserole dish.

300 g chicken thigh fillets, cut into bite-size pieces

2 tablespoons vegetable oil

400 g long-grain rice, washed and thoroughly drained

1 heaped tablespoon very finely shredded ginger

4 dried black mushrooms, soaked in hot water to soften, stems discarded

2 dried Chinese sausages (*lap cheong*), cut diagonally into 1-cm thick slices

1 tablespoon crisp-fried shallots

2 tablespoons finely chopped spring onion

MARINADE

1 tablespoon black soy sauce

1 teaspoon oyster sauce

1 teaspoon Chinese rice wine, preferably Shao Hsing

1 teaspoon sugar

1 teaspoon sesame oil

1. Combine the marinade ingredients in a bowl, stirring to dissolve sugar, then add the chicken pieces. Mix well and leave to marinate for 20–30 minutes.

2. Heat the oil in a large clay pot. Add the rice and stir over medium heat for about 1 minute until the rice is well coated. Add sufficient water to cover the rice by a height of 2 cm. Bring to the boil over high heat, then cook with the pot uncovered for 5 minutes until the water has been absorbed and small craters appear on the surface of the rice.

3. Add the ginger, marinated chicken pieces and mushrooms, pushing well into the rice. Layer the sausages on top, cover and cook over low heat for 20 minutes; do not remove the lid while the rice is cooking.

4. Stir the rice with a fork or chopstick, cover and cook over very low heat for about 15 minutes, until the chicken is done and the rice is dry. Garnish with the crisp-fried shallots and spring onions before serving.

Chicken Biryani Serves 6–8

This favourite Indian Muslim dish, redolent with spices, is one to make when you have plenty of time. Although cooks in India normally use yoghurt, fresh mint and coriander leaf, this Singapore version substitutes coconut milk and curry leaf.

1½ tablespoons chopped ginger

1½ tablespoons chopped garlic

salt as needed

4 tablespoons vegetable oil

2 large onions, thinly sliced

3 tablespoons chicken curry powder, mixed with some cold water into a paste

¼ teaspoon turmeric powder

¼ teaspoon freshly ground black pepper

3 medium tomatoes, skinned and chopped

2 stems curry leaves

600 g boneless chicken pieces (preferably thighs), cut into pieces about 5-cm square

1 cup (250 ml) thin coconut milk

RICE

1 teaspoon vegetable oil

8-cm stick cinnamon

6 cloves

6 cardamom pods, slit and well bruised

1 tablespoon salt

boiling water as needed

800 g Basmati rice, soaked in cold water 30 minutes, well drained

GARNISH

1 tablespoon ghee or butter

45 g raw cashew nuts, halved

fried onions

coriander leaves

1. Process or pound the ginger and garlic with a large pinch of salt to make a paste.

2. Heat 2 tablespoons of the oil in a large pan, then add the onions and cook over low heat for about 15 minutes, stirring often and adding a little more of the oil if needed, until the onions are light brown. Set aside half the fried onions to use as a garnish, leaving the remainder in the pan.

3. Add remaining oil to the pan with the onions, heat, then add the ginger-garlic paste and stir-fry gently for 2 minutes. Add the curry paste, turmeric and black pepper and cook another couple of minutes.

4. Add the chopped tomatoes and curry leaves pulled off their stalk. Raise the heat a little and cook, stirring a few times for 3–4 minutes, until the tomatoes soften.

5. Add the chicken pieces and stir-fry for about 5 minutes until they change colour and are well coated with spices. Add the coconut milk and 1 teaspoon salt and bring slowly to the boil, stirring occasionally. Partially cover the pan, lower the heat and simmer for about 20 minutes until the chicken is just cooked. If there is more than ¼ cup of sauce left in the pan, remove the chicken pieces and simmer to reduce the sauce.

6. Prepare the rice. Heat the oil in a large pan then add the cinnamon, cloves and cardamom and stir-fry for about 2 minutes until the spices smell fragrant. Add the salt and enough boiling water to fill three-quarters of the pan. When the water returns to the boil, slowly add the drained rice in a stream, stirring to prevent the grains clumping together. Lower the heat slightly and boil uncovered until just cooked, no more than 4 minutes, then drain thoroughly in a sieve.

7. Put half the rice and spices into a heavy-bottom pan. Add the chicken and its sauce, then top with the remaining rice. Cover the pan with a clean kitchen towel and the lid. Cook over very low heat for 20 minutes. Turn off the heat and leave to stand for about 10 minutes. (Do not remove the lid.)

8. To make the garnish, heat the ghee in a small pan and gently cook the cashews over low heat, stirring frequently, until golden. Transfer the chicken and rice to a large serving dish, then scatter with the cashews, reserved fried onions and coriander leaves.

Gado Gado Serves 4–6

Known as *gado gado*, which also means riot, this is a substantial mixture of cooked and raw vegetables, fried bean curd and egg, smothered with a peanut sauce and topped with crunchy prawn crisps (*krupuk*). You could use a packaged *gado gado* sauce to save time.

250 g unpeeled small waxy potatoes, boiled

2 cups (500 ml) water

200 g long beans or green beans, cut into 3-cm lengths

200 g cabbage, coarsely shredded

100 g water spinach (*kangkong*), English spinach (*poh chye*) or Ceylon spinach (amaranth)

160 g bean sprouts

$^1/_2$ cucumber

$^1/_2$ teaspoon salt

2 hard-boiled eggs, peeled and quartered

1 piece (100 g) hard bean curd, deep-fried for 3 minutes, sliced

fried prawn crackers (*krupuk*) to garnish

GADO GADO SAUCE

8 large red chillies, sliced

1 teaspoon dried shrimp paste

2 tablespoons vegetable oil

8 shallots, thinly sliced

1$^1/_2$ cups (375 ml) coconut milk

$^1/_2$ cup crunchy peanut butter or 75 g dry-roasted unsalted peanuts, coarsely crushed

1–2 teaspoons crushed palm sugar

1 tablespoon tamarind, soaked in $^1/_4$ cup (60 ml) warm water, squeezed and strained for juice

salt to taste

1. To make the *gado gado* sauce, process the chillies and shrimp paste until finely ground. Heat the oil in a saucepan and stir-fry the shallots over medium heat until softened. Add the chilli paste and cook until fragrant, 4–5 minutes. Add the coconut milk, a little at a time, then add peanut butter or peanuts, sugar and tamarind juice. Bring to the boil, stirring, then lower heat and simmer until the sauce thickens, about 3 minutes. Add salt to taste and cool to room temperature before serving.

2. Peel the cooked potatoes and cut into 1-cm thick slices. Bring water to the boil, add the beans and simmer for 3 minutes. Remove and drain. Cook the cabbage in the same water until just tender, about 3 minutes. Remove and drain. Repeat with the spinach, cooking for 2 minutes only. Blanch the bean sprouts in boiling water for 5 seconds, then drain and plunge into a bowl of iced water to refresh. Drain again.

3. Leave cooked vegetables to cool to room temperature. Scrape the skin of the cucumber with the tines of a fork and massage in the salt for 30 seconds. Rinse under running water, wipe dry and cut the cucumber into 5-mm thick rounds.

4. To serve, arrange the potatoes, vegetables, boiled eggs and fried bean curd in separate piles on a large serving platter. Pour the room-temperature sauce over and garnish with the prawn crackers.

Roti John Serves 4

In the 1960s, a spicy minced meat stew served with sliced French bread (*keema roti*) was very popular among the British Armed Forces stationed in Changi. This combination evolved into *roti* John—bread spread with a layer of minced meat and eggs, then fried. (The name came about because in those days, every Englishman was nicknamed John by the locals.) The British servicemen have long since left, but this substantial snack remains a favourite.

vegetable oil, as needed

1 large onion, finely chopped

1$^1/_2$–2 tablespoons meat curry powder

$^1/_2$ teaspoon chilli powder

$^1/_2$ teaspoon turmeric powder

500 g finely minced lean beef

$^1/_2$–1 teaspoon salt

2 eggs

1 large French loaf, halved lengthways, each half cut across into 4 pieces

chilli or tomato sauce

1. Heat a wok, then add 3 tablespoons oil. Gently stir-fry the onion until it turns transparent. While the onion is cooking, mix the curry powder, chilli and turmeric powders with enough water to make a stiff paste. When the onion has softened, add the spice paste and cook, stirring frequently, 1–2 minutes. Add the meat and cook, stirring from time to time, until the meat is well coloured and any moisture has dried up, about 5 minutes. Add salt and enough water to cover the meat. Bring to the boil, lower heat and simmer until the meat is tender and the liquid has completely dried up. Leave to cool slightly.

2. Break the eggs into a bowl, stir a couple of times to break up the yolks, then stir in the cooked meat. Divide the mixture into 8 portions and spread each piece of bread evenly with some of the meat, pressing down firmly with the back of a spoon so it will not fall off during cooking.

3. Oil a heavy frying pan or griddle generously, then heat. Put 2 or 3 pieces of bread, with the meat side facing down, into the pan and press the top firmly. Cook over high heat until the meat is golden brown, 1–2 minutes. Turn and cook the other side briefly. Add a little more oil and continue until all the slices of bread are cooked. Serve hot with plenty of chilli or tomato sauce.

Roti Prata Makes 8

This light flaky bread (known as *roti canai* across the Causeway in Malaysia) is usually eaten with curry gravy and a thin lentil dip. Skilled *roti* makers have perfected the art of tossing out a ball of dough in ever-increasing circles until it is paper-thin, but most of us have to make do with gently pulling and stretching the dough before cooking it.

325 g plain flour
1 teaspoon salt
1 tablespoon ghee or butter
1 small egg, lightly beaten
$^{1}/_{2}$ cup (125 ml) milk
warm water as required
ghee or oil for coating the dough balls and frying

1. Sift the flour and salt into a large bowl then rub in the ghee or butter. Put the egg and milk into a cup and add sufficient warm water to make 200 ml (just over $^{3}/_{4}$ cup). Make a well in the flour and add the egg mixture, stirring to make a soft dough. Transfer to an oiled board and knead until smooth and elastic, about 10 minutes, adding a little more flour if the mixture seems to be sticky. Alternatively, put all the ingredients in a food processor fitted with a plastic blade and process on low speed for 3 minutes.

2. Divide the dough into 8 balls. Coat the dough balls thoroughly with oil and place in a wide bowl. Cover the bowl and leave in a warm place for at least 1 hour, or overnight.

3. Remove a ball of dough, put on a greased surface, then press to stretch it into a thin oval, about 28 cm x 18 cm. Fold both sides in towards the centre, then pick up the dough and squeeze gently to make a 'rope' at least 30 cm long. Coil the 'rope' into a circle onto a greased tray. Repeat with the remaining dough balls, cover with plastic wrap and leave for at least 30 minutes, or for several hours.

4. Just before cooking, take a coil of dough and squeeze it into a ball. Oil your hands and press to make a circle. Keep pressing all over, pushing the dough out from the centre while gently pulling out the edges with your other hand to stretch it as thinly as possible, until it forms a disc about 25 cm in diameter.

5. Heat 1 teaspoon oil or ghee on a griddle or heavy frying pan. Put in a piece of dough and pour a little more oil around the edges as it cooks to help make it puff up. When the underneath is golden brown, flip over and cook the other side. Serve hot with curry or sugar.

Murtabak Makes 8

Murtabak are made of dough, fried on a griddle and filled with minced meat, onion, egg and sometimes green peas. They are often served with a side dish of sliced cucumber doused with tomato sauce.

250 g plain flour

$1/2$ teaspoon salt

$2/3$ cup (170 ml) warm water

$1/3$ cup (85 ml) vegetable oil

1 large egg, lightly beaten

1 large red or brown-skinned onion, very finely chopped

FILLING

2 tablespoons vegetable oil

1 small red or brown-skinned onion, finely chopped

2 teaspoons smashed and finely chopped garlic

1 teaspoon finely grated ginger

$1/2$ teaspoon turmeric powder

$1 1/2$ teaspoon chilli powder

350 g minced lean lamb or beef

1 teaspoon garam masala

$1/2$ teaspoon salt

1. Sift the flour and salt into a large bowl. Combine water and oil, then add to the flour and mix to make a soft dough. Knead on a floured board for 5 minutes until smooth and elastic. Divide the dough into 8 balls, roll in oil and leave in the bowl. Cover the bowl with plastic wrap and leave in a warm place for 1 hour.

2. Heat oil for filling in frying pan, then stir-fry the onion over low-medium heat for 3 minutes. Add the garlic and ginger and stir-fry for 1 minute. Add turmeric and chilli powders, stir for a few seconds, then add the meat and stir-fry until it changes colour. Cover the pan and leave to simmer for 15 minutes. Sprinkle the garam masala and salt over the meat, stir and cook uncovered for 3 minutes.

3. With greased hands, shape each ball of dough into a circle. Place on a large greased board. Press the dough into a thin circle, then keep pulling around the edges to stretch dough as thinly as possible, until it is about 30 cm in diameter.

4. Grease a large frying pan with a little oil and heat. When the oil is very hot, put in a circle of dough. Smear the dough with 1 tablespoon beaten egg, then scatter one-eighth of the meat filling and one-eighth of the chopped onion over the dough. Fold up envelope-fashion and cook for 2 minutes until golden. Turn and cook the other side. Repeat until all the *murtabak* are cooked. Serve hot; some Indians like to accompany *murtabak* with sliced cucumber sprinkled with bottled tomato sauce.

Seafood

Butter Prawns *46*

Chilli Crab *49*

Black Pepper Crab *50*

Fish Head Curry *53*

Spicy Banana Leaf Stingray *54*

Orr Chien *57*

Yee Sang *58*

Butter Prawns Serves 4

I'm not certain whether this amazing cross-cultural recipe originated in Singapore or Malaysia, but it's been very popular on both sides of the Causeway since the early 1990s. This combination of Chinese cooking styles and ingredients, Indian curry leaves, Malay coconut and bird's eye chillies and Western butter and milk is a winner. Forget the cholesterol and enjoy!

600–750 g large prawns

vegetable oil for deep-frying

1 tablespoon sugar

1 tablespoon Chinese rice wine, preferably Shao Hsing

2 teaspoons light soy sauce

1 teaspoon salt

$1/2$ teaspoon freshly ground black pepper

30 g butter

4–8 red or green bird's-eye chillies, roughly chopped

$1/4$ cup loosely packed fresh or dried curry leaves

1 tablespoon finely chopped garlic

$1/2$ cup freshly grated or desiccated coconut, toasted in a wok until golden brown

$1/4$ cup (60 ml) evaporated milk

1. Wash and drain the prawns. For each prawn, cut off the tip of the head with the feelers, leaving the rest of the head and shell intact. Cut along the back with a sharp knife to remove the dark intestinal tract. Dry the prawns thoroughly with paper towels.

2. Heat a wok, then add oil for deep-frying. When the oil is smoking hot, add a small handful of the prawns and deep-fry for 30 seconds. Remove and drain on paper towels. Cook the remaining prawns in small batches.

3. Combine the sugar, rice wine, soy sauce, salt and pepper in a small bowl and set aside.

4. Discard the oil from the wok, wipe it clean with paper towels, then add the butter. Heat until the butter stops sizzling, then add the chillies, curry leaves, garlic and coconut. Stir-fry over moderate heat until the curry leaves turn crisp, about 1 minute.

5. Add the prawns and the reserved seasoning mixture and stir-fry over moderate-high heat for 1 minute. Add the evaporated milk, stir for a few seconds then transfer to a serving plate.

Chilli Crab Serves 4–6

For special occasions, I like to prepare this version of the chilli crab made popular by seafood restaurants located along the East Coast near Bedok Corner in the 1970s. Some of these restaurants had gardens that led down to the sandy beach and one even kept its live crabs (claws safely tied) in huge baskets under the coconut palms. Although the restaurants have moved, chill crab remains a firm favourite among Singaporeans.

1.5–2 kg live mud crabs

2 tablespoons oil

3 tablespoons very finely chopped fresh ginger

2 tablespoons very finely chopped garlic

3–4 red bird's-eye chillies, finely chopped

1 tablespoon salted soy beans (*tau cheo*), mashed

1 tablespoon Chinese rice wine, preferably Shao Hsing

$^1/_2$ cup (125 ml) bottled tomato sauce

$^1/_4$ cup (60 ml) bottled chilli sauce

1 tablespoon sugar

1 teaspoon salt

$^1/_4$ teaspoon white pepper

1 cup (250 ml) water

1 tablespoon cornflour, mixed with a little water

2 eggs, lightly beaten

sprigs of coriander leaves to garnish (optional)

1. Stun the crabs by putting them in the freezer for 15–20 minutes. Cut in half lengthways with a cleaver, then remove the back shells and spongy grey matter. From the body sections, remove the claws and crack with a cleaver in several places. Cut each body section into 2–3 pieces, leaving the legs attached. Wash, drain thoroughly and pat completely dry.

2. Heat the oil in a wok and add garlic, ginger and chillies. Stir-fry over low–medium heat for about 3 minutes until fragrant, and add the salted soy beans. Stir-fry for a few seconds, then add the crabs and stir-fry for 2 minutes. Add the rice wine, cook for a few seconds, then add the tomato and chilli sauces, sugar, salt, pepper and water. Bring to the boil, then lower the heat and simmer, stirring frequently, until the crabs turn bright red and are cooked, about 10 minutes.

3. Add the cornflour mixture, stirring until the sauce thickens and clears. Add the eggs and stir until set, then transfer the chilli crabs to a serving dish. Garnish with coriander leaves and serve with crusty French bread, if desired.

Black Pepper Crab Serves 4–6

This excellent and easy way of cooking crabs with freshly roasted and ground black pepper is equally good with prawns or slipper lobsters (also known as bugs or crayfish). Adjust the amount of pepper to suit your taste, but be sure to dry-roast it just before grinding for maximum flavour.

1.5–2 kg live crabs or slipper lobsters or 1 kg large prawns

3–4 tablespoons black peppercorns

oil for deep-frying

50 g butter

2 tablespoons very finely chopped garlic

1 tablespoon very finely chopped ginger

1 teaspoon salt

2 tablespoons Chinese rice wine, preferably Shao Hsing

1 tablespoon oyster sauce

1 tablespoon light soy sauce

1 tablespoon sugar

1. Stun the crabs by putting them in the freezer for 15–20 minutes. Cut in half lengthways with a cleaver, then remove the back shells and spongy grey matter. From the body sections, remove the claws and crack with a cleaver in several places. Cut each body section into 2–3 pieces, leaving the legs attached. Wash, drain thoroughly and pat completely dry.

2. Put the peppercorns in a wok and dry-fry over low–medium heat until they start to smell fragrant. Remove and crush coarsely in a mortar or in a spice grinder; do not grind to a fine powder.

3. Heat the oil in a wok and deep-fry the crabs until they turn red, 3–4 minutes. Drain on paper towels and discard the oil. Add the butter to the wok, then stir-fry the garlic and ginger over medium heat until fragrant. Add the pepper, salt and rice wine and stir for about a minute, then add the oyster sauce, soy sauce and sugar, mixing well.

4. Add the fried crab pieces and cook, stirring frequently, for about 5 minutes. Serve with rice or crusty French bread.

If using slipper lobsters, remove the head and halve the body lengthways. If using prawns, trim the feelers and slit the back to remove the dark intestinal tracts before cooking.

Fish Head Curry Serves 4–6

A distinctively Singaporean dish, created by an Indian cook originally from Kerala more than 50 years ago, this has rightly become a Singapore classic. There are many versions, this one based on the curry prepared by a Chinese cook in a Racecourse Road eating shop.

1 large bream or snapper head (about 1.5 kg)

4 teaspoons salt

1/4 cup (60 ml) vegetable oil

1 teaspoon brown mustard seeds

5 cups (1.25 litres) thin coconut milk

85 g tamarind pulp, soaked in 1 cup (250 ml) water, squeezed and strained for juice

1 1/2 tablespoons sugar

3–4 sprigs curry leaves

2 medium red or brown-skinned onions, quartered

3 medium tomatoes, quartered

4–6 small okra (ladies fingers), cut diagonally into 5-cm lengths

SEASONING PASTE

15–20 dried chillies, cut into 2-cm lengths, soaked to soften

8–10 shallots, chopped

3 cloves garlic, chopped

4-cm knob ginger, chopped

SPICE PASTE

2 tablespoons coriander seeds

1 tablespoon cumin seeds

1 tablespoon fennel seeds

1 teaspoon white peppercorns

1/2 teaspoon fenugreek seeds

1 teaspoon turmeric powder

1. Rinse the fish head, then rub all over with 2 teaspoons salt. Cover and refrigerate while preparing the other ingredients.

2. Process all the seasoning paste ingredients in a spice grinder to obtain a smooth paste, adding a little of the 1/4 cup of oil if required to keep the blades turning. Set aside.

3. Put all the spice paste ingredients, except for the turmeric powder, in a small pan and cook over low heat, shaking the pan several times until starting to smell fragrant, 1–2 minutes. Grind to a fine powder in a spice grinder, then transfer to a bowl and add the turmeric powder and enough water to make a stiff paste. Set aside.

4. Heat the oil in a large pan and add the mustard seeds. Fry until they start to pop, then add the seasoning paste and stir-fry over low–medium heat for 4–5 minutes until it is fragrant, then add the spice paste and cook for 2 minutes, stirring several times.

5. Add the thin coconut milk, a little at a time, then put in the tamarind juice, sugar, remaining salt, curry leaves and onions. Bring to the boil, stirring, then lower the heat and simmer uncovered for 5 minutes.

6. Rinse the fish head and add to the pan together with the tomatoes and okra. Simmer uncovered until the fish is tender for 10–15 minutes. Serve hot with white rice.

Spicy Banana Leaf Stingray Serves 6–8

Seafood slathered with a fragrant chilli paste, wrapped in banana leaves and cooked on a hot griddle, has become popular at seafood restaurants all over Singapore. Stingray wings, with their tender mild flesh and lack of bones (they just have cartilage) are particularly popular cooked this way. If you prefer, you could use white fish fillets, slices of cleaned squid or peeled prawns.

1–1.5 kg stingray wings, cut into 4 pieces

1 tablespoon tamarind pulp

4 pieces banana leaf or baking paper,
   cut into 30-cm squares

4 small round green limes (*limau kasturi*)

SEASONING PASTE

10–12 dried chillies, cut into 2-cm lengths,
   soaked to soften, some seeds discarded
   to reduce heat, or 2–2$^{1}/_{2}$ tablespoons
   chilli paste (*sambal olek*)

4 cloves garlic, chopped

1 tablespoon dried prawns, soaked to soften

1 teaspoon dried shrimp paste

2 teaspoons sugar

$^{1}/_{2}$ teaspoon salt

$^{1}/_{4}$ cup (60 ml) vegetable oil

1. Put the stingray pieces on a plate and rub with the tamarind pulp, adding a tablespoon or two of water. Set aside.

2. Prepare the seasoning paste by processing the chillies, garlic, dried prawns, shrimp paste, sugar and salt to a smooth paste in a spice grinder, adding a little of the oil if required to keep the blades turning. Heat the oil in a wok and add the paste. Stir-fry over low–medium heat until fragrant and well cooked, 5–6 minutes. Leave to cool.

3. Rinse the stingray pieces and pat dry. Make a slit along the winged edge of each piece to create a pocket. Push some of the seasoning paste into the slit and smear the rest on both sides of each piece of stingray. Soften the pieces of banana leaf by holding over a gas flame or soaking in boiling water until softened. Put a piece of stingray onto each leaf and wrap firmly to enclose.

4. Heat a hotplate or griddle, or a cast iron frying pan. Put on the banana leaf packets and cook for 4–5 minutes, then turn and cook the other side until the stingray is done, about 10 minutes. Alternatively, cook over a hot grill or under a broiler. Serve the fish on the pieces of banana leaf accompanied by cut limes.

Orr Chien Serves 4

There are a couple of versions of this recipe, one using a lot more egg and resembling an omelette, and this one (which I prefer) made with a very thin batter and just a little egg. I still remember the hawker in the Orchard Road car park (opposite what is now Centrepoint Shopping Centre) and the exquisite sauce he served with his *orr chien* back in the early 1970s. This recipe is the closest I can get to his version of one of my all-time favourite hawker dishes.

80 g tapioca, sweet potato or rice flour

3 tablespoons plain flour

$^1/_2$ teaspoon salt

250 ml (1 cup) water

4 tablespoons vegetable oil

2 tablespoons smashed and finely chopped garlic

4 eggs

1 cup raw oysters, drained

1$^1/_2$ cups (125 g) bean sprouts, washed and drained, tails removed (optional)

4 tablespoons light soy sauce

3 tablespoons chopped spring onions

3 tablespoons chopped coriander leaves

a liberal sprinkling of white pepper

DIPPING SAUCE

3 tablespoons bottled chilli-garlic sauce

1$^1/_2$ tablespoons rice vinegar

$^1/_2$ teaspoon sugar

1 teaspoon light soy sauce

1. Prepare the dipping sauce by combining all the ingredients, stirring to dissolve the sugar. Divide among 4 small bowls.

2. Put both lots of flour and salt into a bowl and gradually stir in water to make a very thin batter. Heat 1 tablespoon oil in a frying pan. When very hot, add one-quarter of the garlic and stir-fry for a few seconds. Pour one-quarter of the batter into the pan and rotate the pan so that the batter forms a lacy pancake.

3. When it starts to set, break an egg over the top, spread with a spatula and leave until the omelette is brown underneath. Turn the omelette over, then scatter the top with one-quarter of the oysters, one-quarter of the bean sprouts, if using, 1 tablespoon soy sauce, 2 teaspoons each of the spring onions and coriander leaves and a dash of pepper.

4. Leave for a few seconds, then break up the omelette with a spatula. Transfer to a plate and keep warm. Prepare 3 more omelettes in the same way. Serve hot with dipping sauce.

Yee Sang Serves 4–6

This unusual salad was once eaten by the Cantonese only between the 7th and 15th days of the Lunar New Year celebration, and when I first came to Singapore, it was available in just one unprepossessing Chinatown restaurant. Now that everyone has discovered just how delicious it is, *yee sang* (or *yu sheng*) is available everywhere throughout the entire month of the New Year season.

125 g white fish or salmon fillet, very thinly sliced

1 medium carrot, very finely shredded

1 small white radish, very finely shredded

$^1/_2$ cup hand-shredded pomelo or grapefruit flesh

1 tablespoon very finely shredded pickled red ginger

1 tablespoon very finely shredded fresh ginger

2 tablespoons finely chopped candied winter melon rind

2 tablespoons canned pickled leek, finely sliced

3–4 kaffir lime leaves (*daun limau purut*), very finely shredded

FLOUR CRISPS

65 g plain flour

1 teaspoon butter

$^1/_4$ teaspoon salt

1 small egg, lightly beaten

SAUCE

2 teaspoons sugar

$^1/_4$ teaspoon white pepper

$^1/_2$ teaspoon salt

$^1/_2$ teaspoon five-spice powder

$1^1/_2$ tablespoons lime juice, preferably from small round green limes (*limau kasturi*)

GARNISH

2 tablespoons coarsely crushed dry-roasted peanuts

1 tablespoon sesame seeds, toasted until golden

1. Prepare flour crisps first by combining all ingredients to make a dough, adding a little more flour if the mixture is too sticky. Roll out as thinly as possible and cut into 2-cm squares. Deep-fry in hot oil until crisp. Drain and when completely cool, store in an airtight container.

2. Arrange all the fish and salad ingredients, flour crisps and garnish on a large serving dish. Place the serving dish in the centre of the table.

3. Put the sauce ingredients into a large bowl, stirring to mix well. As the tossing of the salad is considered essential for good luck in the coming year, everyone should help by tossing the salad with chopsticks. Eat immediately.

Meat & Poultry

Chicken Curry 63

Tandoori Chicken 64

Grilled Chicken 67

Ayam Goreng 68

Lamb, Chicken or Beef Satay 70

Beef Rendang 73

Sop Kambing 74

Bak Kut Teh 77

Chicken Curry Serves 4–6

Many cooks buy prepared curry pastes these days, but if you want to make a traditional version of chicken curry, try this authentic recipe.

¹/₄ cup (60 ml) vegetable oil

1 fresh chicken (1.25–1.5 kg), cut into serving pieces

2¹/₂ cups (625 ml) coconut milk

2 stems lemon grass, bottom 12 cm only, bruised

1 teaspoon salt

SEASONING PASTE

1 tablespoon coriander seeds

2 teaspoons cumin seeds

1 teaspoon fennel seeds

2-cm piece cinnamon, broken

4 candlenuts, crushed

12 shallots, chopped

8–10 dried chillies, cut into 2-cm lengths, soaked to soften

2 teaspoons finely grated ginger

2 teaspoons finely chopped garlic

¹/₂ teaspoon turmeric powder

¹/₄ teaspoon freshly grated nutmeg

1. Prepare the seasoning paste. Toast the coriander, cumin, fennel and cinnamon in a dry pan over low heat for about 1 minute until fragrant. Process to a fine powder in a spice grinder. Add the candlenuts and process until crushed, then add the shallots, chillies, ginger, garlic, turmeric powder and grated nutmeg. Process to a fine paste, adding a little oil if required to keep the blades turning.

2. Heat the oil in a wok for 30 seconds, then add the seasoning paste and stir-fry over low-medium heat for 4–5 minutes. Add the chicken pieces and stir-fry until they change colour and are well coated with the spice paste, about 5 minutes.

3. Add the coconut milk, lemon grass and salt and bring slowly to the boil, stirring constantly. Simmer gently with the wok uncovered, stirring from time to time, until the chicken is cooked and the gravy thickened, 20–25 minutes. Serve hot with steamed white rice.

You can add a few kaffir lime leaves for a Nyonya accent, if you desire.

Tandoori Chicken Serves 4–6

This Northern Indian chicken dish has almost become an international culinary cliché, but that doesn't stop it from being excellent. This recipe was given to me by the late Wadhu Sakhrani, owner of Omar Khayyam in Hill Street, Singapore's first elegant Northern Indian restaurant (alas, long gone).

1 fresh chicken (about 1.25 kg), halved lengthways
3 tablespoons melted ghee or butter
4 lime wedges

MARINADE 1

1 teaspoon salt
1/2 teaspoon turmeric powder
1/2 teaspoon chilli powder
1/4 teaspoon white pepper
a pinch of ground cloves
1 teaspoon crushed garlic
1 1/2 tablespoons lime juice

MARINADE 2

1/2 cup coriander leaves
1/2 cup mint leaves
2.5-cm knob ginger, chopped
1/4 cup (60 ml) plain yoghurt
1 tablespoon cumin powder, preferably freshly ground
1 teaspoon white vinegar
1/2 teaspoon cardamom powder
1/4 teaspoon cinnamon powder
a few drops of red or orange food colouring (optional)

1. Remove the skin from the chicken and make several deep slashes in the thighs and breast to allow the marinade to penetrate. Combine all the ingredients for marinade 1 and rub into the chicken. Refrigerate for at least 3 hours.

2. Put all the ingredients for marinade 2 in a spice grinder and process to a smooth paste. Rub this all over the chicken pieces, making sure to push some of the marinade into the slashes. Refrigerate for at least 6 hours, or overnight, if preferred.

3. Brush the chicken halves all over with the ghee or butter and cook over a hot grill or under a broiler until done, 20–25 minutes. Alternatively, put the chicken pieces on a rack and cook in a pre-heated oven at 220°C for 45 minutes.

4. Cut the chicken halves into serving pieces and serve with lime wedges, a salad or a fresh mint or coriander chutney.

You can buy ready-made tandoori marinade in almost any supermarket today. For a quick and good result, combine the store-bought marinade with yoghurt mixed with some crushed garlic and ginger, and a little salt.

Grilled Chicken Serves 4–6

This simply marinated chicken is usually deep-fried, but I find that it tastes just as good when grilled, and is certainly a healthier choice.

1 kg chicken pieces

2 potatoes, peeled and thinly sliced

1 red onion, very thinly sliced

1 ripe tomato, sliced

¼ cup cooked green peas

MARINADE

1 tablespoon dark soy sauce

1 tablespoon vegetable oil

1 teaspoon salt

1 teaspoon sugar

1 teaspoon ground white pepper

SAUCE

3 tablespoons water

3 tablespoons dark soy sauce

1 tablespoon Chinese plum sauce

1 teaspoon sugar

1–2 tablespoons lime juice

1. Put the chicken pieces in a bowl. Combine the marinade ingredients in a small bowl, then pour over the chicken and rub to coat the pieces well. Set aside for 10 minutes.

2. Heat a grill and cook the chicken, turning over frequently, until golden brown all over and cooked through, 15–20 minutes.

3. While the chicken is cooking, pat dry the potato slices with paper towels. Heat the oil for deep-frying in a wok until hot, then add the potatoes and deep-fry until golden brown. Remove and drain on paper towels. Set aside.

4. Prepare the sauce. Combine the water, soy sauce, plum sauce and sugar in a small saucepan and cook over low heat, stirring constantly until the sugar has dissolved. Stir in the lime juice as desired, and taste to achieve the right balance of sweet and sour. Heat through.

5. When the sauce is ready, arrange the grilled chicken pieces on a serving plate and pour the sauce over. Garnish with the sliced potatoes, onion, tomato and peas. Serve hot.

Ayam Goreng Serves 4–6

It's amazing how a simple seasoning of salt and turmeric brings out the flavour of the chicken in this basic recipe.

1 fresh chicken (1.25–1.5 kg), cut into serving pieces, or 1 kg chicken pieces

2 teaspoons salt

2 teaspoons turmeric powder

vegetable oil for deep-frying

1. Dry the chicken pieces. Combine salt and turmeric powder in a small bowl, then sprinkle over the chicken and rub to coat evenly. Set aside for 5 minutes.

2. Heat oil in a wok and when smoking hot, fry the chicken, a few pieces at a time, until golden and cooked, 4–5 minutes. Drain on paper towels.

3. When all the chicken has been cooked, increase the heat and fry the chicken pieces again until they are brown all over and crisp, about 1 minute. Drain and serve with *sambal belacan* (page 27) or bottled chilli-garlic sauce.

Lamb, Chicken or Beef Satay Makes about 50 sticks

You can use either lamb, chicken or beef to make these famous Malay spiced skewers, or even use a mixture of all three (on separate skewers, of course). These days, it's easy to buy the rich peanut sauce that is the traditional accompaniment to satay. However, it's not difficult to make your own if you have time. I usually opt for crunchy peanut butter instead of the usual crushed peanuts, and to save even more time, you could use 2 tablespoons of crushed chilli or *sambal olek* instead of dried chillies.

1 tablespoon coriander seeds

1 teaspoon cumin seeds

1/2 teaspoon fennel seeds

8 shallots, chopped

2 cloves garlic, chopped

1 stem lemon grass, tender part of bottom 10 cm only, thinly sliced

1-cm knob galangal, chopped

1-cm knob ginger, chopped

11/2 teaspoons salt

2 teaspoons palm sugar

1 tablespoon tamarind pulp, soaked in 1/4 cup (60 ml) warm water, squeezed and strained for juice

1/2 teaspoon turmeric powder

1 kg boneless lamb leg, boneless chicken thigh or rump steak, cut into 1.5-cm cubes

50 bamboo skewers

vegetable oil for brushing

2 medium red or brown-skinned onions, each cut into 10–12 wedges, to garnish

1 cucumber, halved lengthways, cut diagonally into 2-cm thick pieces, to garnish

SATAY SAUCE

8 dried red chillies, cut into 2-cm lengths, soaked to soften

8 shallots, chopped

1 clove garlic, chopped

4 candlenuts, chopped

1 stem lemon grass, tender inner part of bottom 10 cm only, thinly sliced

2 tablespoons vegetable oil

1 cup (250 ml) coconut milk

1/2 cup crunchy peanut butter or 75 g dry-roasted unsalted peanuts, coarsely crushed

1 tablespoon tamarind pulp, soaked in 1/4 cup (60 ml) warm water, squeezed and strained for juice

1 teaspoon brown sugar

salt to taste

1. Prepare the satay sauce. Process or pound the chillies, shallots, garlic, candlenuts and lemon grass to a smooth paste.

2. Heat oil in a saucepan and add the chilli paste. Stir-fry over low–medium heat until fragrant, 4–5 minutes. Add the coconut milk and bring to the boil, stirring constantly.

3. Add the peanut butter or peanuts, tamarind juice and sugar. Simmer gently for 2–3 minutes. Add salt to taste and thin with a little boiled water if desired. Leave to cool to room temperature before serving.

4. Put the coriander, cumin and fennel seeds in a small pan and cook over a low heat, shaking the pan several times, until the spices smell fragrant. Process to a fine powder in a spice grinder, then set aside.

5. Process the shallots, garlic, lemon grass, galangal, ginger, salt and palm sugar to a fine paste in the spice grinder, adding a little of the tamarind juice if required to keep the blades turning.

6. Put the ground spices, shallot mixture, tamarind juice and turmeric powder in a large bowl, stirring to mix well. Add the meat and stir to coat well. Cover and refrigerate for at least 4 hours, or leave overnight if preferred, stirring several times.

7. Soak the bamboo skewers in water for about 30 minutes to help prevent them from burning during grilling. Thread several pieces of meat onto each skewer and brush with oil. Grill, preferably over charcoal, turning, until the meat is cooked and golden brown all over, 5–8 minutes.

8. Serve satay with the onions, cucumber and satay sauce for dipping.

Beef Rendang Serves 4–6

Rendang is full of fragrance and flavour, even though most versions (including this one) do not contain dried spices. Adding kaffir lime leaves seems to be a more recent practice among some Singapore Malays, though the use of turmeric and *kerisik* (pounded toasted coconut) are both traditional. Turmeric leaves are often hard to obtain, but the *rendang* still tastes good if you have to omit them.

4 cups (1 litre) coconut milk

1¹/₂ teaspoons salt

1 teaspoon sugar, or more to taste

4 kaffir lime leaves (*daun limau purut*)

2 fresh turmeric leaves, torn into 3 or 4 pieces (optional)

2 stems lemon grass, bottom 12–14 cm only, bruised

1 slice *asam gelugor* or 2 teaspoons tamarind pulp, soaked in 2 tablespoons water, squeezed and strained for juice

600 g topside beef, cut into 4-cm x 1.5-cm thick squares

SEASONING PASTE

12 dried chillies, cut into 2-cm lengths, soaked to soften

12 shallots, chopped

4 cloves garlic, chopped

3-cm knob galangal, chopped

2-cm knob ginger, chopped

2-cm knob fresh turmeric, chopped, or ¹/₂ teaspoon turmeric powder

1. To make the seasoning paste, process all the ingredients in spice grinder until fine, adding a little coconut milk if required to keep the blades turning.

2. Put the seasoning paste, coconut milk, salt, sugar, kaffir lime leaves, turmeric leaves, if using, lemon grass and *asam gelugor* or tamarind juice, into a wok and bring slowly to the boil, scooping up the liquid with a ladle and pouring it back constantly to help prevent it from curdling.

3. Add the meat and simmer uncovered, stirring from time to time, until tender and the coconut milk has greatly reduced, about 1 hour.

4. Discard the leaves and lemon grass and keep cooking until the oil separates from the coconut milk and the meat starts to fry, about 10 minutes. Serve hot with rice.

Sop Kambing Serves 4–6

This substantial Indian dish is traditionally enjoyed as a late night snack with cubes of bread dipped into the rich broth. Leg or shoulder bones with plenty of marrow are the best choices, but any mutton or lamb on the bone will do.

750 g mutton or lamb on the bone, such as shoulder, leg or ribs

3 tablespoons vegetable oil

2 large red or brown-skinned onions, halved lengthways, thinly sliced across

3 tablespoons meat curry powder

1/4 teaspoon fennel powder

6 cups (1.5 litres) water

1 teaspoon salt or more to taste

SEASONING PASTE

15 shallots, chopped

6 cloves garlic, chopped

3-cm knob ginger, chopped

WHOLE SPICES

5-cm piece cinnamon

6 cardamom pods, slit and bruised

5 cloves

1 teaspoon black peppercorns, cracked

1 star anise

GARNISH

2–3 tablespoons crisp-fried shallots

a few sprigs Chinese celery or coriander leaves

white pepper to taste

lime wedges

1. Remove as much fat as possible from the meat. If using shoulder chops, cut each piece with a cleaver into 2–3 pieces. Process all ingredients for the seasoning paste until finely ground. Tie all the whole spices in a piece of clean muslin or cheesecloth.

2. Heat the oil in a large pan and add the onions. Stir-fry over low–medium heat until they start to turn light brown, then add the seasoning paste and stir-fry for 3–4 minutes, until it starts to smell fragrant; add a little more oil if the mixture starts to stick. Mix the curry and fennel powders together with enough water to make a paste, then add to the pan and stir-fry for 1 minute.

3. Add the meat, water, salt and bag of whole spices. Stir well and bring to the boil. Lower the heat, cover the pan and simmer for about 1 1/2 hours, until the meat is tender. Remove the spice bag.

4. Serve the soup in large bowls garnished with shallots, celery or coriander leaves and white pepper. Accompany with pieces of French bread. Squeeze a little fresh lime juice over the soup.

If you want to reduce the amount of fat to the minimum, leave the soup to cool, then chill until the fat sets on the surface; this can be spooned off and discarded. The soup can be prepared a day ahead as it keeps well.

Bak Kut Teh Serves 4

Singapore cooks used to go to a Chinese medicine store to get the appropriate herbs for this nourishing soup. These days, packets of herbs for *bak kut teh* are sold in just about every supermarket. For a change, you could try the Nyonya version, using whole spices rather than medicinal herbs.

500 g meaty pork ribs

2 small heads garlic, left whole and unpeeled

6 cups (1.5 litres) water

2 teaspoons salt

1 1/2 tablespoons dark soy sauce

1 packet *bak kut teh* spices or Nyonya spice blend (see below)

NYONYA SPICE BLEND

5-cm piece cinnamon

6 cloves

2 points star anise

1/2 teaspoon white or black peppercorns

1/2 teaspoon coriander seeds

1/2 teaspoon cumin seeds

1/2 teaspoon fennel seeds

1. Put the pork ribs, garlic, water, salt, dark soy sauce and *bak kut teh* spices in a large saucepan, adding more water if needed to cover the meat. If using Nyonya spice blend, tie the cinnamon, cloves, star anise, peppercorns, coriander, cumin and fennel seeds in a small piece of clean muslin or cheesecloth and add to the pan. Bring to the boil, lower the heat and simmer for 5 minutes.

2. Remove any scum that has risen to the top and discard. Lower the heat, partially cover the pan and simmer very gently until the meat is very tender. Remove the heads of garlic, and the bag of spices.

3. Transfer the soup and ribs to 4 bowls, and accompany with sauce dishes of sliced large red chillies in dark soy sauce, if desired. Serve with sliced Chinese deep-fried savoury crullers (*yu char kway*) or steamed white rice.

Light Meals & Snacks

Chye Tow Kuey *80*

Popiah *82*

Otah Otah *85*

Taukwa Goreng *86*

Rujak *89*

Vadai *90*

Curry Puffs *93*

Goreng Pisang *94*

Kuih Dadar *97*

Chye Tow Kuey Serves 4–6

This is one of my favourite hawker dishes and now that I live in an area where Teochew dishes are impossible to find, I cook it myself. You need to start preparations well in advance because you must make the radish cake first, unless you live in Singapore where you often find the ready-made cake in the local supermarkets.

300 g large white radish (*lobak*), coarsely grated

1 heaped teaspoon salt

2 tablespoons vegetable oil or lard

2 teaspoons sesame oil

4–5 shallots, sliced

2–3 dried black mushrooms, soaked to soften, caps thinly sliced

3 tablespoons dried prawns, soaked and coarsely ground

2 teaspoons light soy sauce

$1/4$ teaspoon white pepper

180 g rice flour

40 g tapioca flour

$2^{1}/_{2}$ cups (625 ml) cold chicken stock

FOR FRYING

3 tablespoons vegetable oil

4 cloves garlic, smashed and finely chopped

1 heaped tablespoon chopped salted radish (*chye poh*)

2 eggs

2–3 teaspoons light soy sauce

2–3 teaspoons chilli paste (*sambal olek*)

1 spring onion, finely chopped

1. Mix the grated white radish with the salt in a bowl and set it aside to draw out some of the moisture.

2. Heat both lots of oil in a medium pan, then gently fry the shallots and mushrooms until the shallots turn golden. Add the dried prawns and fry until they smell fragrant, 2–3 minutes. Sprinkle with soy sauce and pepper, stir-fry for a few more minutes, then transfer to a bowl. Squeeze the radish to remove the moisture, then add to the bowl and stir to mix well with the fried ingredients.

3. Before transferring the saucepan to the stove, put in both lots of flour and stir in the chicken stock. Put over low–moderate heat and bring slowly to the boil, stirring constantly until the mixture thickens—do not leave the mixture unattended for even a moment or it may become lumpy. Stir in the reserved radish mixture, mixing vigorously (the mixture will be thick and heavy), then transfer to a greased 24-cm heatproof dish, levelling the top with a spatula.

4. Put in a steamer or on a rack set above boiling water in a wok, cover and steam, adding hot water to the steamer from time to time, for 1 hour. Leave until cold, then refrigerate for at least an hour, or up to several days, before the final stage. (This makes almost 1 kg of cooked radish cake.)

5. You may need to do the final frying in 2 batches unless you have a really large frying pan. Heat 2 tablespoons oil in a wide heavy frying pan. When it is very hot, add the radish cake, breaking it up with a wok spatula and turning it until golden all over. Push to the side

of the pan, add another tablespoon of oil and cook the garlic and salted radish until the garlic is soft and fragrant.

6. Break in the eggs, leaving to set slightly before sprinkling over the soy sauce and vigorously pushing the eggs around to combine with the radish cake. Add chilli paste to taste, stir again, then transfer to serving dish.

7. Sprinkle the spring onion over the cake and serve with additional white pepper and fresh chilli sauce, if desired.

If you have any left-over cooked *chye tow kuey*, you can reheat it in a pan with very hot oil and a handful or two of bean sprouts for a variation in flavour.

Popiah Serves 4–6

There's no denying that these delightful fresh spring rolls take time to make, but if you're entertaining, all the work can be done well in advance. Fresh spring rolls skins, which do not contain egg, are very difficult to make at home, so I've developed an alternative recipe for the wrappers.

2 tablespoons chilli paste (*sambal olek*)

8 cloves garlic, crushed to a paste with a little salt

4 tablespoons *hoisin* sauce

12 long-leaf lettuce leaves, torn into halves

100 g shredded cucumber

150 g bean sprouts

1 piece (100–125 g) hard bean curd, deep-fried until golden, finely diced

2 hard-boiled eggs, peeled and coarsely chopped

2 Chinese sausages (*lap cheong*), simmered in water for 3 minutes, thinly sliced

WRAPPERS

125 g plain flour

$1/2$ teaspoon salt

$1^1/4$ cups (300 ml) water

5 eggs, lightly beaten

2 teaspoons vegetable oil

COOKED FILLING

1 tablespoon oil

1 small red or brown-skinned onion, thinly sliced

2 cloves garlic, finely chopped

$1^1/2$ tablespoons salted soy beans (*tau cheo*), lightly mashed

100 g pork loin or fillet, shredded

100 g prawns, peeled and heads removed

250 g canned bamboo shoot, shredded

250 g yam bean (*bangkwang*), shredded, or additional 250 g bamboo shoot

1 tablespoon light soy sauce

1. Make the wrappers first. Put flour and salt in a bowl and stir in the water to make a smooth batter, then add eggs. Heat a 20-cm frying pan, add $1/2$ teaspoon oil and swirl to grease thoroughly. Add $1/2$ cup batter and swirl the pan to spread it in a thin layer. Cook over moderate heat until set, for 30 seconds. Turn and cook other side. Stack on a serving plate and repeat until the batter is used up.

2. Heat oil for the cooked filling in a large saucepan. Stir-fry onion and garlic over low heat until soft, then add salted soy beans and stir-fry for 1 minute. Raise the heat, put in pork and stir-fry until it changes colour, about 1 minute. Add prawns and stir-fry for 1 minute, then put in bamboo shoot, yam bean and soy sauce. Stir the mixture, bring to the boil, then reduce heat. Cover and simmer very gently for 30 minutes, adding 1 tablespoon water from time to time if the mixture seems to be drying out. Transfer the mixture to a bowl and cool to room temperature.

3. Just before serving, transfer the cooked filling and the plate of cooked wrappers to the dining table. Put the chilli paste, garlic and *hoisin* sauce in small sauce bowls on the table. Arrange the lettuce leaves, cucumber, bean sprouts, bean curd, boiled eggs and Chinese sausages on a large plate. Each person takes a wrapper and smears it with chilli paste, garlic and *hoisin* sauce to taste. A lettuce leaf is put on top, then some of the cooked filling and other ingredients. Tuck in both sides and roll up like a cigar. The rolls can be sliced into 3–4 bite-size pieces, if preferred.

Otah Otah Makes 14–15 parcels

This Nyonya-style mixture of highly seasoned fish is normally wrapped inside coconut leaves for grilling over charcoal. As coconut leaves are now pretty difficult to find in Singapore or any other big city, I recommend using banana leaf, baking paper or even aluminium foil. This recipe makes 14–15 parcels; double the amounts if serving a crowd.

500 g white fish fillets, skinned and boned

1/2 cup (125 ml) thick coconut milk

1 teaspoon salt

1 1/2 teaspoons sugar

1/2 teaspoon white pepper

banana leaf, cut into 14–15 pieces,
    each 16 cm x 24 cm

SEASONING PASTE

1 1/2 medium onions, chopped

6 dried chillies, cut into 2-cm lengths,
    soaked to soften

2 cloves garlic, chopped

1-cm knob fresh turmeric, sliced, or
    1/2 teaspoon turmeric powder

3 candlenuts, chopped

1 stem lemon grass, tender part of bottom
    8 cm, thinly sliced

1 tablespoon chopped polygonum leaves
    (daun kesom)

1 1/2 teaspoons coriander seeds, lightly
    toasted and ground

1. Prepare the seasoning paste by processing all the ingredients to a fine, smooth paste, adding a little of the coconut milk if needed to keep the blades turning. Set aside.

2. Cut the fish into cubes, then pulse in a food processor until coarsely minced. Add the coconut milk, salt, sugar, pepper and seasoning paste and pulse to obtain a smooth paste. If possible, refrigerate for at least 30 minutes to firm up the mixture.

3. Soften the pieces of banana leaf by holding above a gas flame, or soaking in boiling water until softened.

4. To make a parcel, place a piece of leaf lengthways and dark, shiny side down on the working surface. Add about 2 heaped tablespoons of the fish mixture, flattening it slightly to make it about 1-cm thick. Fold the leaf over a few times to firmly enclose the filling and secure both ends with toothpicks. Repeat until the fish mixture is used up.

5. Grill, preferably over charcoal, for 3–4 minutes on each side. Serve with rice or as a snack; the *otah otah* can even be used as a sandwich filling.

The *otah otah* can be kept in a plastic box and stored in the freezer for up to a month. To serve, thaw completely before grilling.

Taukwa Goreng Serves 4–6

This bean curd dish is a popular snack at Malay food stalls. Usually, the whole bean curd cake is cut diagonally and a slit made on one side of each triangle so that it can be filled with the cucumber and bean sprouts, but this is an easier method.

vegetable oil for deep-frying

4 cakes (about 400 g) hard bean curd, dried with paper towels

1 small cucumber

2 teaspoons salt

160 g bean sprouts, washed and drained, tails removed

SAUCE

4 shallots or $^{1}/_{2}$ large red-skinned onion, chopped

2–3 large red chillies, chopped

$^{1}/_{3}$ cup (80 g) chunky peanut butter

2 tablespoons finely chopped palm sugar or soft brown sugar

4 teaspoons dark soy sauce

1 tablespoon tamarind pulp, soaked in $^{1}/_{4}$ cup (60 ml) water, squeezed and strained for juice

$^{1}/_{4}$ teaspoon salt

$^{1}/_{4}$ cup (60 ml) water

1. Prepare the sauce by processing the shallots and chillies in a spice grinder until finely ground, adding a little water if required to keep the blades turning. Add the peanut butter, sugar, dark soy sauce, tamarind juice and salt, then process until just well mixed. Alternatively, pound to a smooth paste in a mortar. Transfer to a bowl and gradually add water to make a thick sauce. Set aside.

2. Heat the oil in a wok. Add the bean curd and deep-fry for about 4 minutes until golden brown and crisp on both sides. Drain on paper towels, then cut into 1-cm thick slices.

3. Rake the skin of the cucumber with a fork, then rub well with salt. Rinse under running water, squeeze the cucumber, then cut into matchstick strips. Arrange the bean curd on a serving plate, top with the cucumber strips and bean sprouts. Pour the sauce over and serve immediately.

Rujak Serves 4–6

There are many versions of this dish. At its simplest, it combines under-ripe fruits such as mango, papaya and pineapple with cucumber and a pungent sweet-sour sauce. Singaporean Chinese usually add yam bean (sometimes called jicama), water spinach, bean curd, bean sprouts and Chinese savoury crullers (*yu char kway*), and at times even cured cuttlefish.

1 small cucumber, skin raked with a fork

1 small yam bean (*bangkwang*), peeled

1–2 small unripe mangoes, peeled and sliced, or 1 cup sliced half-ripe papaya

1 thick slice under-ripe pineapple, cut into bite-size pieces

1 piece deep-fried brown bean curd (*tau pok*) or 1 piece (100 g) hard bean curd, deep-fried until golden brown and cut into large cubes

80 g bean sprouts, scalded in boiling water for a few seconds

a small bunch water spinach (*kangkong*), simmered until soft, cut into 5-cm lengths

1 deep-fried savoury cruller (*yu char kway*), cut into 2-cm slices (optional)

75 g dry roasted peanuts, coarsely crushed

2 tablespoons white sesame seeds, toasted until golden brown

a few slices torch ginger bud (*bunga kantan*), finely minced

SAUCE

4 tablespoons black shrimp paste (*hay koh*)

3 tablespoons finely chopped palm sugar

1/2 teaspoon dried shrimp paste, toasted

2–3 teaspoons crushed chilli

1 tablespoon dark soy sauce

1 tablespoon tamarind pulp, soaked in 1/4 cup (60 ml) water, squeezed and strained for juice

1 tablespoon lime juice, preferably from small round green limes (*limau kasturi*)

salt to taste (optional)

1. To prepare the sauce, put the black shrimp paste in a bowl and stir in the palm sugar and dried shrimp paste until dissolved. Add the chilli and dark soy sauce, then slowly stir in the tamarind and lime juices. Taste and add salt if desired.

2. Cut the cucumber and yam bean into small wedges and put in a large bowl with the mango, pineapple, bean curd, bean sprouts and water spinach. Pour over the sauce and toss, then transfer to a serving dish or bowl and scatter with savoury cruller, if using, peanuts and sesame seeds. Finally, sprinkle all over with some finely minced torch ginger, if using, and serve immediately.

For easy handling, you may prefer to cut the savoury cruller and deep fried brown bean curd with a pair of kitchen scissors, like hawkers selling *rujak* always do.

Vadai Makes about 18 small pieces

This really tasty Southern Indian snack, usually found in vegetarian restaurants, is not difficult to make. However, you do need to soak the lentils overnight, and a food processor is essential for grinding them into a paste.

300 g husked black gram lentils (*urad dhal*)

2–3 large green chillies, sliced

1 medium red or brown-skinned onion, coarsely chopped

1-cm knob ginger, chopped

1 sprig curry leaves

1 teaspoon salt

rice flour as required

vegetable oil for deep-frying

1. Immerse the lentils with water to cover overnight.

2. Process the chillies, onion, ginger and curry leaves until finely chopped then remove and set aside. Drain the lentils, add to a food processor and grind into a smooth paste, adding up to 3–4 tablespoons water as required to keep the blades turning. Transfer to a bowl and stir in the chilli mixture and salt. If the mixture seems too wet, add 1–2 tablespoons rice flour.

3. Oil your hands and a plate. Shape the mixture into balls, then flatten slightly and place on the oiled plate. When the mixture is used up, heat oil in a wok.

4. Deep-fry the savouries, a few at a time, over moderate heat, turning until cooked and golden on both sides, about 5 minutes. Drain and serve hot or at room temperature.

Curry Puffs Makes about 24 pieces

There are many recipes for this popular snack. My favourite used to be known as Rex curry puffs, named after the old cinema which stood opposite the open-fronted restaurant famous for its curry puffs. This version of those fondly remembered curry puffs has a filling of chicken and egg rather than the usual spicy minced beef, and is seasoned with roasted curry powder for a very special flavour. (You could use regular curry powder if you're in a hurry.)

250 g plain flour, sifted
1/4 teaspoon salt
100 g chilled butter, diced
1 egg, lightly beaten
2–3 tablespoons iced water
vegetable oil for deep-frying

FILLING
4 teaspoons roasted curry powder (see note below) or regular meat curry powder
2 teaspoons water
1 1/2 tablespoons vegetable oil
1/2 teaspoon finely chopped garlic
1/2 teaspoon finely chopped ginger
100 g boneless chicken thigh or breast, cut into 1-cm cubes
1 cup (250 ml) coconut milk
3/4 teaspoon salt
3 hard-boiled eggs, peeled and each cut into 8 wedges

1. Prepare the filling first. Combine the curry powder with water to make a paste. Heat oil in a wok and stir-fry the garlic and ginger over low-medium heat for about 1 minute. Add the curry paste and stir-fry for 1 minute. Add the chicken, stir-frying until it changes colour and is covered with spices, 3–4 minutes. Add the coconut milk and salt. Bring to the boil, cover and simmer until cooked, about 10 minutes. Transfer to a bowl to cool.

2. Pulse the flour, salt and butter in a food processor until the mixture resembles breadcrumbs. Add the beaten egg and water and process until the mixture forms a ball of dough. Place dough in a plastic bag and refrigerate for 30 minutes.

3. Roll out the dough on a floured board until about 5-mm thick, then cut into 10-cm circles. Put 1 tablespoon filling and 1 piece of egg in the centre of each circle. Wet the circumference of the dough with a finger dipped in water, then fold one edge over to form a semi-circle. Twist the edges to seal. The curry puffs can now be refrigerated or even deep-frozen until required.

4. Heat oil for deep-frying in a wok. Fry the curry puffs, a few at a time, over medium heat, turning to brown each side, 4–5 minutes altogether. Drain on paper towels and serve warm or at room temperature. (If cooking frozen curry puffs, do not defrost but add them directly to the oil and cook for 6–7 minutes.)

To make roasted curry powder, put 1/4 cup coriander seeds, 4 teaspoons cumin seeds, 1 teaspoon each of brown mustard seeds and cardamom seeds, 2 cloves and 2-cm piece cinnamon (broken) in a saucepan. Cook over low heat, shaking the pan frequently, until the spices are fragrant and lightly browned. Grind to a fine powder in a spice grinder. When cool, the mixture can be kept refrigerated in a tightly closed jar for many months.

Goreng Pisang Makes 8

I have never understood why this popular snack is called *goreng pisang* in Singapore, rather than the correct Malay name, *pisang goreng*. The batter, which contains lime or alkaline water, can also be used for coating the pungent fruit, cempedak, slices of sweet potato and yam. Lime or alkaline water ensures a really crisp texture for the batter and is available in Chinese stores and many supermarkets.

125 g plain flour

80 g rice flour

2 teaspoons baking powder

a pinch of salt

1 teaspoon powdered lime (*kapur*), mixed to a paste with a little water or 2 tablespoons alkaline water (optional)

1 cup (250 ml) water

vegetable oil for deep-frying

8 large, firm ripe bananas, peeled

1. Sift both lots of flour, baking powder and salt into a bowl. Add the lime paste or alkaline water, if using. Gradually stir in the water to make a thick batter.

2. Heat the oil for deep-frying in a wok. Dip the bananas into the batter, turning to coat thoroughly. When the oil is very hot, add the battered bananas and fry until golden brown, about 4 minutes. Drain thoroughly and serve warm.

Kuih Dadar Serves 4–6

These Malay pancakes are scrumptious and can be enjoyed at any time of the day.

3 *pandan* leaves, cut into 5-cm lengths, or a few drops of *pandan* essence

¹/₄ cup (60 ml) water (if using *pandan* leaves)

1 cup (125 g) plain flour

a pinch of salt

1 egg, lightly beaten

2 cups (500 ml) milk

a few drops of green food colouring (optional)

2 tablespoons vegetable oil

FILLING

60 g finely chopped palm sugar

¹/₄ cup (60 ml) water

100 g grated coconut

1. If using fresh *pandan* leaves, put in a blender with the water and process until crushed. Strain through a sieve and press down with the back of a spoon to extract as much of the bright green juice as possible. Set aside.

2. Sift the flour and salt into a bowl. Make a well in the centre and add egg, milk and reserved *pandan* juice. Mix to make a smooth thin batter, adding a little more milk if required, to obtain the consistency of cream. Add *pandan* essence and food colouring, if using.

3. Prepare the filling by heating the palm sugar and water in a small saucepan, stirring until dissolved. Add the coconut and stir over low heat for 1 minute. Spread out on a plate to cool.

4. Lightly grease a 15-cm diameter frying pan, preferably non-stick, with about ¹/₂ teaspoon oil, swirling to grease the bottom of the pan. Pour out any excess oil. Heat until medium-hot.

5. Add almost ¹/₄ cup pancake batter, swirling to spread over the bottom of the pan. Cook for about 45 seconds until set underneath, then flip to cook the other side for 30–45 seconds. Stack on a plate and continue until the batter is used up.

6. When the pancakes are cool, put 2 tablespoons coconut filling in the centre of each pancake. Fold up the end closest to you to cover the filling, tuck in the sides and roll up to enclose the filling firmly. Serve at room temperature.

Glossary

Asam Gelugor

ASAM GELUGOR
The Malay name for these brown slices of dried fruit is often inaccurately translated as tamarind slices. In fact, this souring agent has nothing to do with tamarind (*Tamarindus indica*) but comes from two types of Garcinia fruit. The thick dark brown slices sometimes sold are more sour than the thinner, lighter-coloured variety, which is more widely available. *Asam gelugor* is often preferred for adding to fish dishes, although regular tamarind juice can be used as a substitute.

BANANA LEAVES
Few Singaporeans now live with a banana tree in the garden, but packets of cut fresh banana leaves can still be bought in markets and some supermarkets (and in many Asian markets in the West). These serve as wrappers for steamed or grilled food, adding moisture and a touch of flavour as well as protecting the food within. After cutting a banana leaf into the desired size, soften by holding it briefly above a gas flame, or put in a bowl of boiling water until softened. Drain and pat dry. Make sure the shiny side of the leaf is outside when enclosing the food. If banana leaves are not available, wrap with baking paper and, if you are worried that it might unravel, wrap with an extra layer of aluminium foil.

DEEP-FRIED BROWN BEAN CURD (TAU POK)
Better known in Singapore as *tau pok*, deep-fried brown bean curd has been compressed, cut into cubes and deep-fried over high heat so that it becomes light and spongy inside. When added to stews or the popular *laksa* dish, the cubes absorb the tasty liquid. Before adding to dishes, blanch in boiling water for about a minute to remove excess oil.

BLACK SHRIMP PASTE
This should not be confused with dried shrimp paste, as it has a very different flavour and texture. A black, very thick paste sold in jars, this is sometimes labelled "black prawn paste", "*otak udang*" or "*petis*", while the Chinese name is *hay koh*. It is used in some sauces and added to a few Penang-style dishes.

Dried Red Chillies

CHILLIES, DRIED
These dried chillies are made by sun-drying large ripe (red) chillies. Several different varieties are imported to Singapore, and they vary in intensity. Dried chillies are often preferred to fresh red chillies for the brighter colour they give to curries, and for their different aroma. Dried chillies should be cut into small pieces and soaked in hot water to soften before grinding or processing, discarding some of the seeds if you want to keep the flavour and colour, but reduce the spiciness. Crisp dried chillies can be coarsely ground to make chilli flakes, used as a condiment.

CHINESE CHIVES
Also known as Chinese or coarse chives, these garlicky-tasting green blades are used as a herb; when the flower buds develop, they are cooked as a vegetable. Spring onions can be used as a substitute.

Chinese Sausages

CHINESE SAUSAGES (LAP CHEONG)
Mottled reddish sausages, generally sold in pairs, these are scented with rose-flavoured rice wine. They are used primarily as a flavouring, particularly with rice or noodles. They keep without refrigeration.

Curry Leaves

Dried Prawns

CURRY LEAVES

There is no substitute for these small, dark green leaves from the *karuvapillai* tree, used mostly by Southern Indian and Sri Lankan cooks, but also popular among Singapore Malays for fish curry. Dried curry leaves make an acceptable substitute; fresh curry leaves keep very well in the freezer.

DRIED PRAWNS

These dried small, pinkish-orange prawns (shrimps) are used as a seasoning and not as a substitute for fresh prawns. They are often soaked in lukewarm water before using to soften and remove any preservatives. Do not use hot or boiling water as it removes much of the flavour.

grill directly over a medium gas flame or under a grill. Cook for about 2 minutes, then turn and cook the other side for another few minutes. Open the packet to check that the shrimp paste has lost its wet, raw look and smells fragrant. Alternatively, put the foil package into a heated wok or non-stick frying pan; it may take a little longer to cook.

GALANGAL

Known as *lengkuas* in Malay, this member of the ginger plant has a distinctive fragrance redolent of the jungle. Slices of fresh galangal can be deep-frozen for future use if a regular supply is not available. Water-packed galangal from Thailand (sometimes simply labelled "rhizome" or *khaa*) makes an acceptable substitute.

HOISIN SAUCE

A sweetish red-brown sauce sold in jars, used in marinades or dipping sauces in Chinese cuisine.

Dried Black Mushrooms

Dried Shrimp Paste

Kaffir Lime Leaves

DRIED BLACK MUSHROOMS

These are very important as a seasoning and a vegetable in Chinese cuisine, the dried mushrooms developing a much more intense flavour than the fresh (often sold under their Japanese name, *shiitake*). Very thick and crinkled mushrooms, sometimes known as flower mushrooms, take much longer to soak than the normal flat dried mushrooms. Cover with hot water and leave for 20–30 minutes for normal mushrooms or overnight for flower mushrooms.

DRIED SHRIMP PASTE (BELACAN)

This pungent paste, known locally as *belacan*, adds an intensity to many local dishes, particularly the popular condiment known as *sambal belacan*. It varies in colour from very dark brown through to a purplish pink, and should be toasted to remove the raw taste. To do this, put the required amount on a piece of foil, folding over a flap and pressing down to make a thin layer. Tuck the edges of foil in loosely to make a packet, then set this on a wire

KAFFIR LIME LEAVES

One of the most popular herbs among Nyonya cooks, and recognisable by its double leaves; it is normally known in Singapore by the Malay name, *daun limau purut*. If you can buy the fresh leaves, store them in a bag in the freezer; the dried leaves are a poor substitute. In most recipes, you could substitute $1/4$ teaspoon grated lime or lemon rind for 1 kaffir lime leaf. Fresh kaffir lime leaves are often finely shredded for adding to salads and other dishes. Roll up the leaves from the tip to stem, like a cigar, then lay on a board and use a sharp knife to cut into hair-like shreds, discarding the hard central rib.

LEMON GRASS

Important in Malay and Nyonya cuisine, lemon grass (*serai*) looks rather like a miniature leek. The coarse blade-like leaves are normally discarded and only the bottom 8–10 cm of the stem used. The stem is usually pounded for seasoning pastes or lightly bruised before being added whole to simmering food. Peel away several of the outer layers to get the tender inner portion if you are processing lemon grass to a paste, or if using the slices raw in a dip or salad. Lemon grass can be kept for a few weeks by putting the stems in about 1 cm of water in a glass, and set in a warm, sunny place such as by a kitchen window. Add water from time to time; roots will eventually sprout, and if you want to grow your own lemon grass, transfer it to the garden or a pot at this stage. If fresh lemon grass is not regularly available, thinly sliced deep-frozen lemon grass, sold in packets (or prepared at home when you have plenty of fresh lemon grass on hand), can be substituted; 1 tablespoon sliced lemon grass

is roughly equivalent to the tender bottom portion of one stem.

Small Round Green Limes (Limau Kasturi)

LIMES

Two types of lime are used to give a fruity sour tang to many dishes: the larger round yellow-skinned lime or *limau kapas* and the small, round bright-green fragrant lime, *limau kasturi* (or *kesturi*). The latter is often known abroad by its Filipino name, *kalamansi*, or as *calomondin* (from the botanical name, *Calomondin mitis*). The bumpy skinned kaffir lime is used not for its juice (for it scarcely has a drop) but for its very fragrant zest, which is grated into some Nyonya dishes. Substitute lemon zest if this is not available. (Incidentally, whole kaffir limes can be kept in the freezer and grated while still frozen.)

NOODLES

Introduced by the Chinese, but adopted by all Singaporeans, noodles come in many varieties, both fresh and dried. Fresh noodles should be refrigerated until used; dried noodles will keep almost indefinitely in a cool, dry cupboard.

- **Fresh rice flour noodles** are sold either cut into flat strands about 1 cm in width (known as *kway teow* or *hor fun*), or made into spaghetti-like round noodles which are preferred for *laksa*. Fresh rice noodles have

been steamed before being sold; blanch in hot water for about 1 minute before using, drain and use as directed.

- **Dried rice vermicelli** (*beehoon*) is very fine rice flour noodles. Dried rice stick noodles (also known as rice ribbon noodles) are flat and vary in width from about 3 mm to 1 cm and are used primarily in dishes of Thai origin. Dried rice flour noodles should be soaked in hot water for about 10 minutes to soften. They are then generally boiled until cooked, which will take 30–60 seconds for rice vermicelli or 3–5 minutes for rice stick noodles, depending on the thickness.

- **Fine or medium fresh wheat noodles** should be shaken to dislodge any starch (used to stop them from sticking together) and blanched in boiling water for up to 1 minute to cook. Rinse under cold water and drain.

- **Hokkien noodles** are thick, fresh and yellow-coloured wheat noodles. Blanch in boiling water for about 1 minute to remove any oil or impurities. Drain and use as directed in the recipe.

- **Dried wheat noodles,** a good substitute for the fresh varieties, are normally boiled without any pre-soaking; the cooking time will depend upon the thickness, but is usually around 3 minutes (check the time stated on the package). Separate with a long fork or chopsticks during cooking, and once cooked, rinse in cold water and drain. If this last step is omitted, the noodles may become gluey. Varieties with added egg are sometimes labelled "egg noodles".

Pandan Leaves

PANDAN LEAVES
The blade-like leaves of the fragrant screwpine (*daun pandan*) plant add a wonderful fragrance to some desserts and are also used in some savoury dishes. *Pandan* essence and green food colouring can be substituted in cakes, but if fresh *pandan* leaves are not available where required for wrapping food or for adding to savoury dishes, omit from the recipe.

Polygonum

POLYGONUM
This is the botanical name for a very pungent herb commonly called laksa leaf in Singapore (because it is usually added to this noodle dish), and it may also be known by its Malay name, *daun kesom*. In the West, this herb is sometimes called Vietnamese mint or long-stemmed mint, although the flavour is quite different to true mint.

Salted Soy Beans

SALTED SOY BEANS
This seasoning is made from fermented salted soy beans, and normally sold in jars. Some brands have added sugar or chillies, so check the label before buying. The beans, ranging in colour from pale yellow to rich brown, are packed in a thick liquid; the beans either left whole or mashed. Some Chinese brands are labelled "Yellow Bean Sauce" but in Singapore, this is generally referred to as *tau cheo* or *tau cheong*.

TAMARIND
The dried brown pulpy seeds extracted from the ripe pods of the huge tamarind tree adds a touch of fruity sourness to many Malay, Nyonya and Indian dishes. The tamarind used in these recipes is unrefined tamarind pulp, complete with seeds (Thai brands are very good). If you are using cleaned tamarind (sold in jars), with the seeds and fibres removed, reduce the amount of tamarind specified in these recipes by about half. I do not recommend the use of tamarind concentrate, which does not seem to have a good flavour and is often hard to dissolve. To make tamarind juice, put the specified amount of tamarind pulp in a bowl and add warm water as directed. Soak (do not rinse) for about 5 minutes, then squeeze with your fingers and remove any seeds and coarse fibres. Pour the pulp and liquid through a fine sieve, pressing down firmly to extract as much juice as possible. (See *Asam gelugor* for "tamarind slices".)

Torch Ginger Bud

TORCH GINGER BUD
The beautiful pink bud of the torch ginger—*bunga kantan* or *bunga siantan*—is added to salads or cooked in soups and curries. When cooked with fish, torch ginger bud has a flavour and fragrance somewhat reminiscent of polygonum. There is no substitute for this; if you are able to obtain the fresh buds, you can freeze them whole for future use.

TURMERIC
A member of the ginger family, this rhizome gives a vivid yellow colour and fragrance to Malay and Nyonya dishes. Fresh turmeric leaves are used as a herb in some Malay and Indonesian dishes. If fresh turmeric rhizome is available, it should be scraped and then processed or pounded as directed, bear in mind that it was a traditional yellow dye for fabrics and avoid getting the juice on clothing.

Weights & Measures

Quantities for this book are given in Metric and American (spoon and cup) measures. Standard spoon and cup measurements used are: 1 teaspoon = 5 ml, 1 tablespoon = 15 ml, 1 cup = 250 ml. All measures are level unless otherwise stated.

LIQUID AND VOLUME MEASURES

Metric	Imperial	American
5 ml	$1/6$ fl oz	1 teaspoon
10 ml	$1/3$ fl oz	1 dessertspoon
15 ml	$1/2$ fl oz	1 tablespoon
60 ml	2 fl oz	$1/4$ cup (4 tablespoons)
85 ml	$2^1/2$ fl oz	$1/3$ cup
90 ml	3 fl oz	$3/8$ cup (6 tablespoons)
125 ml	4 fl oz	$1/2$ cup
180 ml	6 fl oz	$3/4$ cup
250 ml	8 fl oz	1 cup
300 ml	10 fl oz ($1/2$ pint)	$1^1/4$ cups
375 ml	12 fl oz	$1^1/2$ cups
435 ml	14 fl oz	$1^3/4$ cups
500 ml	16 fl oz	2 cups
625 ml	20 fl oz (1 pint)	$2^1/2$ cups
750 ml	24 fl oz ($1^1/5$ pints)	3 cups
1 litre	32 fl oz ($1^3/5$ pints)	4 cups
1.25 litres	40 fl oz (2 pints)	5 cups
1.5 litres	48 fl oz ($2^2/5$ pints)	6 cups
2.5 litres	80 fl oz (4 pints)	10 cups

DRY MEASURES

Metric	Imperial
30 grams	1 ounce
45 grams	$1^1/2$ ounces
55 grams	2 ounces
70 grams	$2^1/2$ ounces
85 grams	3 ounces
100 grams	$3^1/2$ ounces
110 grams	4 ounces
125 grams	$4^1/2$ ounces
140 grams	5 ounces
280 grams	10 ounces
450 grams	16 ounces (1 pound)
500 grams	1 pound, $1^1/2$ ounces
700 grams	$1^1/2$ pounds
800 grams	$1^3/4$ pounds
1 kilogram	2 pounds, 3 ounces
1.5 kilograms	3 pounds, $4^1/2$ ounces
2 kilograms	4 pounds, 6 ounces

OVEN TEMPERATURE

	°C	°F	Gas Regulo
Very slow	120	250	1
Slow	150	300	2
Moderately slow	160	325	3
Moderate	180	350	4
Moderately hot	190/200	370/400	5/6
Hot	210/220	410/440	6/7
Very hot	230	450	8
Super hot	250/290	475/550	9/10

LENGTH

Metric	Imperial
0.5 cm	$1/4$ inch
1 cm	$1/2$ inch
1.5 cm	$3/4$ inch
2.5 cm	1 inch

Although a New Zealander by birth, the late Wendy Hutton spent the majority of her life in Southeast Asia, becoming an acknowledged authority on the region's food. She was perhaps best known for her books on Singapore cuisine, having authored the ground-breaking *Singapore Food* (first published in 1979), *The Food of Love* (on Eurasian cuisine), and *Green Mangoes and Lemon Grass* among other titles.

After she moved from Singapore to Sabah, Malaysian Borneo, Wendy went on to write more than a dozen books on Borneo's natural environment. She travelled widely in Asia, enthusiastically exploring local cuisines and returning to Singapore as often as possible to enjoy what she regarded as some of the world's best food.

MORE ON SINGAPORE CUISINE

Singapore Heritage Cookbooks

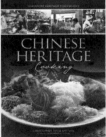 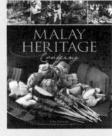 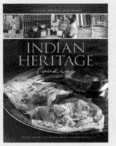  

Chinese Heritage Cooking
ISBN 978-981-4346-44-3

Malay Heritage Cooking
ISBN 978-981-4328-66-1

Indian Heritage Cooking
ISBN 978-981-4346-45-0

Eurasian Heritage Cooking
ISBN 978-981-4346-46-7

Peranakan Heritage Cooking
ISBN 978-981-4346-47-4

The Best of Singapore's Recipes

Everyday Favourites
ISBN 978-981-4276-02-3

Festive Cooking
ISBN 978-981-261-867-2

Hearty Meals
ISBN 978-981-261-868-9

Hot & Spicy Treats
ISBN 978-981-261-866-5

Nyonya Specialties
ISBN 978-981-4276-03-0

Teatime Delights
ISBN 978-981-261-869-6